DERBYSHIRE GROUNDS
A POST-WAR SURVEY

Simon Lacey, Chris Higginbottom
and Tom Whittington

Published by Simon Lacey

ISBN: 0-9547056-0-2

Authors: Simon Lacey, Chris Higginbottom,
Tom Whittington © 2004

Published by Simon Lacey

Printed by Irongate Digital Solutions, Derby

We can ask and ask but we can't have again what once seemed ours for ever...They've gone and you can only wait for the pain to pass

J.L.CARR ('A Month in the Country')

To Derek Sederman

in recognition of his

contribution to the

Robin Hodgkin memorial

service

20th June 2004

Steve Fairclough

CONTENTS

FOREWORD

By Jon Salisbury (Chairman of the Derbyshire Cricket Board)

GHOSTS IN THE LANDSCAPE

When I was a child I went with my father to Derby Congregational C.C. on Brayfield Road in Littleover. Even as a child I knew that it was an important place to be. It was the anticipation before the game that drew me in. The game was filled with rituals; the whites; the sporadic knock-up on the outfield; the banter with opponents; and the procession of the captains to the middle to make the toss. Even Test players played at Congs. I can remember Michael Frederick appearing there only three of four years after he played for the West Indies against England. He changed in the railway carriage like everyone else. It was my first acquaintance with the possibility of stirring deeds about to be performed; of fifties scored and applauded; of bowlers delivering with raw speed or with guile and subtlety; and of the slowly building tension as a game unfolded. This could be so excruciating that it was scarcely possible to keep watching. It was all so addictively compelling.

I have always been drawn to a sense of what has gone before. It is probably why I ended up teaching history. I am fascinated by change brought about by people; by those who worked the land or those whose sweat and effort went into radical changes of the landscape – the canal and railway builders in particular. What of those who played on the land? Cricket for me is the best of games – enjoyable, fascinating and skilled. It is a game played on grounds of various shapes and sizes in so many villages and communities throughout the county. What dramas were enacted on those grounds sometimes no more than farmers fields with a moderately cared for bit in the middle. Changing rooms could be old railway carriages with no facilities to speak of. All the kit that was needed was found in a large, leather club bag. Such grounds were theatres of a full range of human emotions. There was the atmosphere of the gentleman's game with its striped blazers, 'jazz hats' and its 'play-up and play the game' philosophy but there was also the full passion of brute force, sublime skill, temper tantrums, gracious behaviour and downright cheating.

It was always impossible to know how games would unfold. Some events would be talked about for years afterwards and slowly merge into the folklore of the game in the local area. It is that which fascinates me about cricket grounds. They all have their individuality and their histories that are utterly unique. They all offer the promise of ghosts flitting across the turf re-enacting games of days gone by. This book will encourage your own memories of grounds where you might smile in silent recognition of achievements, sights and experiences fondly remembered.

ILLUSTRATIONS

Crowden
Tintwistle
Hadfield
Glossop
Charlesworth
Moorfield
Hayfield
Birch Vale
New Mills
Edale
Castleton
Hope
Bamford
Buxworth
Chinley
Whaley Bridge
Chapel-en-le-Frith
Hathersage
Peak Forest
Dove Holes
Peak Dale
Grindleford
Eyam
Tideswell
Calver
Burbage
Buxton
Baslow
Great Longstone
Taddington
Chelmorton
Ashford in the Water
Chatsworth
Sterndale Moor
Bakewell
Flagg
Monyash
Rowsley
Stanton in Peak
Youlgreave
Darley Dale
Birchover
Friden
Elton

County of Derbyshire
Northern Map

5 Kilometres

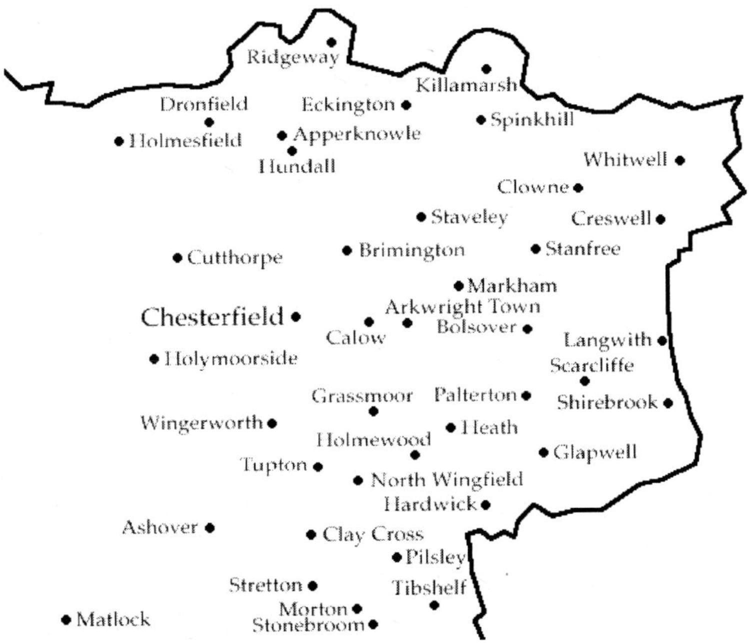

Bonsall
Cromford
Middleton
Longcliffe
Parwich
Wirksworth
Carsington
Hopton
Tissington
Idridgehay
Ashbourne
Turnditch
Clifton
Osmaston
Weston Underwood
Norbury
Brailsford
Shirley
Kedleston
Abbotsholme
Kirk Langley
Longford
Doveridge
Sutton on the Hill
Sudbury
Etwall
Burnaston
Hilton
Hatton
Egginton
Willington
Repton
Newton
Solney
Stanton
Swadlincote
Drakelow
Woodville
Church Gresley
Walton-on-Trent
Rosliston
Linton
Overseal
Netherseal
Lullington

County of Derbyshire Southern Map

ACKNOWLEDGMENTS

This book sprang from a crackpot notion. To pass the long winter Saturdays without cricket, I decided to visit every town, village or hamlet in Derbyshire. This idea was slightly modified by the publication of Peter Wynne-Thomas' book about Nottinghamshire cricket grounds. Having decided that Derbyshire ought to have a companion volume, I enlisted the help of two experts. Chris Higginbottom knows an awful lot about Derbyshire cricket and the people who run its clubs and Tom Whittington had access to a digital camera, an almost unfathomable ability to read Ordnance Survey maps and a working knowledge of trees and geology.

We would like to thank the following for their help and assistance: Jill Banks (National Trust at Kedleston), Ian Battersby, George Barton, Keith Breakwell, Pete Brookes, James Cokayne, Pete Collins, Barry Cook, Joan D'Arcy, Stephen Eyre, John Flower, Neil Gilliver, John Grainger, Malcolm McDonough, Ted Paine, Roy Pearce, Derrick Pounds, David Rawlinson, H.Robinson (Blue Circle at Hope), Jon Salisbury, Ronnie Silk, Derek Slack, Chris Springalls, the Sturgess Brothers at Netherseal, Ray Sturt and the patient staff of numerous Derbyshire libraries. The overhead photograph of West Park was very kindly supplied by Multimap, whose excellent website was often useful in identifying lost grounds.

We are painfully aware that this book is not definitive and we would welcome any information on grounds that we have missed or additional information on the grounds we have noted. The authors may be contacted via Shipley Hall Cricket Club, The Field, Shipley, Heanor, Derbyshire DE7 7JH. Any profit from the publication of this book will bc contributed to the building fund of Shipley Hall C.C. in gratitude for the many happy hours we have spent at that lovely ground.

Simon Lacey
West Hallam 2004

INTRODUCTION

As Clint Eastwood says in one of his typically taciturn roles, "A man's gotta know his limitations", so we decided to *only* consider post-war grounds that have been used for senior cricket i.e. between teams principally composed of men and/or women over the age of eighteen. 'Beer' matches played on the local public park or football ground do not qualify in this respect. We have tried to consider all the grounds in context. It would be completely unreasonable to compare grounds like Darley Playing Fields with, for example, Chesterfield or Elvaston. We have also tried to eliminate the bitterness of uncongenial personal experiences from the text.

Derbyshire County Cricket Club has played upon fourteen grounds at first class level. Four of them are not within the bounds of the county itself. The 'foreign' grounds are three at Burton-on-Trent in Staffordshire (Ind Coope, Bass and the Town Ground) and Abbeydale Park at Dore, an ancient Derbyshire village swallowed up by the South Yorkshire city of Sheffield before the war. The principal venues have been the County Ground at Derby and Queens Park, Chesterfield (last used by Derbyshire in 1998 although the M.C.C. played a first class game there in 2002) with a substantial number of games at The Park, Buxton (last used in 1996) and the Rutland Recreation Ground, Ilkeston (last used in 1994). Solitary games over one hundred years apart were played at the current grounds in Heanor and Wirksworth and the grounds of Glossop C.C. and Blackwell M.W.C.C. were used as a consequence of the financial clout of local businessmen before the First World War. Blackwell, in particular, would be unlikely to stage a Derbyshire Under 11 fixture these days, let alone a full county game. Long Eaton Recreation Ground, was used only once (in 1887) and eventually became the Speedway Stadium. Saltergate, the current ground of Chesterfield F.C., was used in 1874 before the establishment of Queens Park. First Eleven limited overs matches have been staged at thirteen different venues; Derby, Chesterfield, Ilkeston, Buxton and Heanor as above; within the county boundaries at Darley Dale, Trent College and Repton School; and over the border in Staffordshire at Burton-on-Trent (Ind Coope ground only), Cheadle, Checkley, Knypersley and Leek. The County Ground, more commonly known in local circles as The Racecourse, has been considerably altered over the years although the square is probably where it stood when the ground was first used in 1871. After many years of biting criticism from players about the open, windswept and weather-beaten conditions, the ground is more enclosed than it has ever been. This is more to do with the sale of land around the pitch to outside interests (Virgin Leisure for example) than any great development plan on the part of the almost permanently cash-strapped county club. It is an unpopular venue within the first class game and is hardly more popular with local players (the prestigious Derbyshire Cup Final has been staged at Denby and, more recently, Chesterfield). It is highly likely that if county cricket survives then Derbyshire will never venture beyond the County Ground again unless a rich patron or local council offers financial inducements to play at an out ground. A detailed description of all the grounds discussed above may be found in the main section of the book with the exception of the 'foreign' grounds, the Speedway Stadium in Long Eaton and Saltergate in Chesterfield (it is unlikely that cricket has been played on either of the latter grounds since the First World War).

To examine the post war developments of local cricket grounds, we have split them into seven groupings and a statistical survey may be found in Appendix B.

1) Grounds that are owned or leased by a private club
2) Grounds that are part of a public park or shared with other sports
3) Grounds established by collieries or miners welfares (although all the mines have gone, a high proportion of their grounds remain)
4) Grounds established by companies
5) Grounds established by institutions (i.e. hospital, church and military grounds)
6) Grounds established by educational establishments (schools, colleges)
7) Grounds associated with a country house (i.e. originally used by the household)

Derbyshire has lost over half the cricket grounds that have been played on since the Second World War. Most of the losses are evenly spread among the categories above, however the loss of company cricket grounds has been grievously widespread. Where once over fifty grounds of this type existed, only thirteen remain. Two of them are not currently used for club cricket (Exchem at Alfreton and Drakelow Power Station) and must be regarded as in danger of disappearing and at least one other (Clay Cross Works) is under threat of sale to the highest bidder that will assuredly not be the sports team that plays there. The decline of company grounds is not just a consequence of greed or financial necessity; although it would be foolish to discount these powerful factors; but also the reluctance of modern cricketers to represent their works rather than the place they live. Also, the modern club cricketer is more mobile than his 1950's counterpart and more willing to switch clubs to play at a higher standard or on a better ground. Even the well-appointed and expertly maintained Rolls Royce ground does not attract more than a moderate team these days. Company grounds are also the most likely to have been built over and this is understandable when one considers that these types of grounds were usually situated in urban locations where land is at a premium.

It is pleasing to note that the majority of grounds that have been lost are either used for other sports (mainly football) or have reverted to green pastures. Many small village grounds were little more than a field donated by a kindly farmer with a quick mow and roll in the middle to provide an invariably vicious playing surface. These grounds were undoubtedly home to poor cricket on poor wickets. They are not to be mourned by those who appreciate that the game must be played on properly prepared surfaces with suitable facilities such as practice nets, showers and toilets if it is to attract young people in the future. This argument also holds good for those public parks that could not meet modern standards (the rarely used Darley Playing Fields are the last remnant of this type of ground).

It is true that some smaller clubs are falling by the wayside but they have been replaced by extra teams run by the stronger clubs. For example, Denby C.C., Lullington Park C.C. and Ockbrook & Borrowash C.C. have four teams each and they have all built second pitches to accommodate their growing membership. Other clubs with more than two teams are also contemplating second pitches or utilise public parks that otherwise would fall into disuse. Here we suspect modern cricketers are more inclined to tolerate poor grounds if they feel they are only there on a temporary basis until promotion to a higher team playing on a better ground.

Visiting the grounds that have stood the test of time will surely give those interested in the well being of cricket many reasons to be cheerful. Pavilion and practice facilities on some of the most rustic grounds are astonishingly good (three cheers for lottery handouts). Thanks to the Derbyshire County League in particular, who have insisted on minimum standards supported by extensive marking schemes for many years, Derbyshire club cricketers have never before played on such consistently well-maintained and well-appointed grounds.

GAZETTEER

ABBOTSHOLME

Abbotsholme School

Like other fee-paying establishments in the county, Abbotsholme School clearly places cricket in a position of some importance and they hosted numerous matches for Derbyshire 2nd XI throughout the 1990's. The ground is some way from the school buildings within the meander of the River Dove. Since this river marks the county boundary, a number of cricketers must have enjoyed the pleasure of hitting a ball out of Derbyshire. The spacious, almost square, cricket field, first used in 1890, is surrounded by four football pitches but they do not intrude onto the outfield that is perfectly level and in excellent condition. The pavilion is a large wooden building and was paid for and constructed by former pupils in 1962. It replaced a smaller structure built by pupils in 1892. A two-storey scorebox, opened in 1968, is opposite the pavilion. Next to the pavilion is a motor shed and toilet block partially hidden by two mature trees. Further along the boundary are two concrete practice strips though they are not enclosed by a permanent net structure. The school can just be seen through trees.

ALDERWASLEY

Packhorse Road, Alderwasley Hall

Belper Oberon C.C. were exiled from their original ground in Belper (see the Belper section for details) in 1959 and leased a field in Alderwasley. The club changed their name to Belper Amateurs and played friendly cricket away from home for three years until their new ground was ready. Despite the best efforts of tree planting around the boundary (predominantly Silver Birch) this is a bleak and open ground. Given good weather, the ground has a desolate beauty but it is murderously uncomfortable in cold conditions. The turf is in good condition and the playing surface is quite level. The pavilion is on the opposite side of the ground to Packhorse Road and was rebuilt in brick after a burglar set fire to the original pavilion in 1977.

There is a concrete net in one corner of the ground and a caravan in the opposite corner shielded by conifers.
The Alderwasley village team used to play close to Alderwasley Hall and the Church of St Margaret. The Hall is now a private school and the ground does not have a square (it is a football pitch owned and used by the school). There is a wooden pavilion of modern design and construction that did not exist when village cricket was played here. There are magnificent parkland views on all sides and the Alderwasley war memorial is alongside the pitch.

ALFRETON

Alfreton Park, Watchorn Park, Mortimer Wilson School, Carnfield Hill

Alfreton Park is a pleasant cricket ground. A sturdy, wood-barred fence encircles the playing area situated on the side of a hill. The whole ground, including the square, markedly slopes from the pavilion at the top. The pavilion is a modern brick building, an unappealing structure for such a pretty ground. The separate wooden scorebox is to the left. The square has an artificial strip on one end but the old concrete practice surface is still in the middle of the outfield and ought to be removed. There are numerous trees around the ground (a solitary horse chestnut is actually inside the fence).
Until they moved to Alfreton Park in the 1960's, Alfreton Miners Welfare C.C. used to play at Watchorn Park on Colliery Road. Robert Watchorn was an Alfreton boy who emigrated to America, made a fortune and became the town's best-known benefactor. He built a church, a library and, in 1927, established the park. The cricket ground has been cut down to accommodate the A38 and is now a football pitch and a children's playground. The small brick pavilion still remains in a corner but the windows have been concreted. This was once an idyllic place to play cricket but now the traffic roars over the boating lake and pleasure grounds that were next to the cricket ground.
The flat and featureless playing fields of Mortimer Wilson School were used by the Alfreton O.B's team from the late 1960's until 1978. There are no permanent structures such as a scorebox, or changing facilities excepting those in the main school buildings.

Exchem, an explosives manufacturer, have their own private ground located outside the factory gates next to the entrance drive towards the M1 at Carnfield Hill. This is a small, rough looking ground last used in 2000 for 3rd XI cricket.

AMBERGATE

Hurt Arms, RJN

There are two grounds in Ambergate and only a field separates them. The ground of Ambergate C.C. is behind the Hurt Arms and is a dried out riverbed given by the Hurt family to their estate workers to "enjoy in perpetuity the game of cricket". Indeed, the arch of the bridge is still exposed on the straight boundary opposite the pub. The boundaries are formed by high stone walls along the main road and as a consequence are extremely irregular. The pavilion, built in 1994 and dedicated to Harry Holmes, is on the bank opposite the road. This is a large stone-faced building with a pitched roof and a verandah in front. The wicket is in the centre of a bowl in the middle of the ground. The straight boundaries are lengthy at their widest points but the square boundaries are very short and sharply sloping on both sides.

The Ambergate Sports and Social Club ground, owned by LB Plastics Ltd, can be glimpsed through trees but is a quarter of a mile by road. This ground is much larger than what is considered the main ground down the road and is unique in Derbyshire having two large rivers alongside (the Amber and the Derwent). The ground has been called the Show Ground but is more commonly known as RJN (Richard Johnson & Nephew Company). The social club is next to the car park alongside the main road and there is a sharp drop down onto the playing surface. An ugly portakabin and shabby wooden changing rooms in front of the football pitch are divided by swings. The cricket pitch is on the far side nearest the Derwent and the outfield on the riverside has not been repaired since silt was deposited in large quantities by the river flooding in the winter of 2000-01. Given the large, even playing surface and the beautiful backdrop of mature woodland this really ought to be the main ground in Ambergate. As it is, it remains a neglected expanse used only by 3rd XI's and friendly teams on Sundays.

APPERKNOWLE

High Street

Apperknowle Cricket Ground was opened in the 1920's. It is a great and ghastly ground in equal measure. The ground is perched on the side of a hill and the humps and hollows down the slope are incredible. There is a particularly stomach churning drop onto the tiny square. The small oval-shaped playing area could actually be bigger if the club utilised the scrubland on two sides. There is a concrete practice strip level with the square on the South East boundary. The pavilion is constructed from several structures attached to form a single whole, raised off the ground on bricks. Part of this building was formerly used in a P.O.W camp. The completely unhindered views from the pavilion are breathtaking. At each end of the ground, across High Street, both God and mammon are close at hand for a tired cricketer after a game. To the left is the Methodist Church and to the right is the Travellers Rest Public House.

ARKWRIGHT TOWN

Colliery Ground

Arkwright Town was built by the Staveley Colliery Company around the dawn of the twentieth century. The cricket ground was probably established soon after because a team representing the town was playing in the Chesterfield & District League by 1911. The ground was square and banked on three sides. It was to the West of the town with railway lines on two sides. In fact, the whole town was completely encircled by railway lines. Cricket ceased here in the 1960's and the town was destroyed and reconstructed in a different location after methane gas leaks in 1988. The area occupied by the cricket ground is now a huge hole created by extensive opencasting works that have excavated around four million tons of coal and simultaneously released the trapped methane gas.

ASHBOURNE

Recreation Ground, Queen Elizabeth Playing Fields

The two cricket grounds of Ashbourne are close neighbours. The Recreation Ground was formerly known as the War Memorial Ground (the gates to the park are situated on Cokayne Avenue) and is a large expanse of parkland catering to a number of sports. The cricket field is forced to yield one side of the outfield to a football pitch and the other side to a rugby pitch. An unbroken line of trees marks the bottom boundary with Henmore Brook gurgling behind. The top boundary is a bank on which three pavilions stand. To the right is the green wooden building that was the old cricket pavilion. This is now used as a store. In the middle is the rugby pavilion with a pitched roof. The cricketers now use the glass-fronted building to the left with a taller scorebox attached on one side. The ground was levelled in the 1960's as a prelude to the West German football team training here prior to the 1966 World Cup.

Behind the rugby pitch is a steep bank and this leads up to the Queen Elizabeth Playing Fields, formerly the grammar school pitches. They were established in 1925 on land purchased from the trustees of the late W.R.Holland and the School Governers kindly allowed the local town club to use the ground. There are beech and hawthorn hedges along the straight boundaries. Next to the car park, the Philip Allen 'Spag' Harries Pavilion is a functional but uninspiring structure built in 1995. The square is in the middle of the field but is flanked by a football pitch and, on the pavilion side, a hockey pitch. Neither appears to be used enough to cause great problems to the outfield and this ground is now only used for 3rd XI cricket. Both Ashbourne cricket grounds are completely level but the turf is rather rough.

ASHFORD IN THE WATER

Mill Lane

Ashford in the Water is the village often pictured on 'Beautiful Derbyshire' calendars. The cricket ground is on Mill Lane before you reach the village. Although the ground is not quite so picturesque as the village, it is very attractive. The pavilion is nestled in the corner nearest the main road on a small incline. In the opposite corner is a splendid sycamore tree. Both the pavilion and scorebox are dedicated to long-standing club members (Alan Cookson and J.A.Hickman respectively). There is a concrete artificial strip behind the pavilion in a distressed condition. One side of the ground is lined with a dry stone wall and the other by a wire fence. The shape of the ground was distorted in the 1960's when a large chunk of outfield was used as part of the new main road. An article in the High Peak News in 1958 suggested that this ground could be the oldest continuously used venue in the county; "...it is undoubtedly true that the club owes much of its popularity to its picturesque ground known by the name of the Hall Croft – or, as it was known when the club was first formed over 117 years ago, Brewell Croft..."

ASHOVER

Grange Farm, Milken Lane

Since the war, Ashover C.C. have played on two grounds, directly opposite each other on Milken Lane. The first of them, a vast triangular field owned by Grange Farm, was first played upon in the 1930's but the club were asked to vacate the ground and moved across the road to the current council-maintained facility next to the showground in 1955. The outfield of the cricket ground also forms part of two football pitches and there are tennis courts and a community centre alongside the car park. The large pavilion, opened in 1974, is diagonally opposite the community centre and is built from timber with stone foundations. The original, crude wooden changing rooms were heavily damaged by a falling tree. A disused artificial net surface runs to one side of the pavilion. The playing area is large but dips away from the pavilion (quite sharply towards the community centre corner). A dry stone wall forms two boundaries but otherwise the ground is quite dull.

ASTON-ON-TRENT

Playing Fields

Aston-on-Trent could be nice. It is located in an attractive village and the ground is lined with trees with the church poking out of the greenery in the background but the ugly, brick pavilion appears scruffy and lovelorn and the nets are in a state of disrepair. The club claims a foundation date of 1860 and it is possible that the ground does date from this period. The pavilion is of more recent vintage and was opened in 1970 by D.B.Carr of Derbyshire and England, who occasionally played for the club when he lived in the village. The ground is owned by the Parish Council and is easily spotted from Shardlow Road.

BAKEWELL

Rutland Recreation Ground

The Rutland Recreation Ground, situated on Haddon Road (the main road North into Bakewell), was not opened until 1884 but a cricket club had been established in the town since 1861. The whole recreation ground comprises approximately thirteen acres and was given to the local council by the Duke of Rutland in 1921. There is a path separating the cricket ground from tennis courts, a football field and a playground with seats along this boundary. The attractive black and white timber pavilion is on the opposite side of the ground with the River Wye running behind. It was paid for by a former president of the club, Mr Stanley Orme and was opened by the Duke of Devonshire in 1929. The public toilets on the ground are nicely disguised behind a seated shelter. Another football pitch borders the pitch to the South. An artificial strip is detached from the rest of the square.

BAMFORD

Recreation Ground

Bamford with Thornhill Recreation Ground is a large open space that currently houses two football grounds, a playground and a running track with a further undeveloped scrubland area in one corner. The River Derwent runs behind the pavilion and must be crossed via a wooden bridge to access the ground down Water Lane. At the entrance is a car park from which a path runs in front of the handsome, and rather neglected, cream and black timber pavilion. The railway line running parallel to the southern boundary is the main Manchester-Sheffield line. The club that played here after the war was poignantly known as Bamford & Derwent C.C. Derwent was the village submerged by a reservoir. The Derwent cricket ground was lost underneath the waters with the rest of the village but it seems that some of their players were absorbed into the Bamford club.

BARROW UPON TRENT

Sinfin Lane

Before the Second World War there was a cricket field off the main road to Swarkestone but when the club was re-formed after the war they played next to a market garden. Unfortunately they had a disagreement with the farmer who owned the land and the club disbanded in the 1950's. The oak pavilion was used by the farmer as a chicken house. The site of the ground is now part of the East Midlands Self Storage depot.

BASLOW

Nether End

Baslow Sports Field at Nether End is a multi-purpose facility. The club and ground were formed around 1910 as an offshoot of Chatsworth C.C. who were unable to offer all their members a regular game. The ground is still owned by the Chatsworth Estate and the original Baslow pavilion, opened in 1933, was very similar to the one still extant at Chatsworth Cricket Ground. There are tennis courts around the imposing stone-built Cavendish Sports Pavilion, opened in 1997, and the football pitch is next to the car park in front of the pavilion. The cricket pitch is on the far side with trees to the left and straight ahead (the main road is unobtrusively to the right). There is a commodious artificial practice surface in the far right hand corner of the ground. The River Derwent flows behind the far boundary. This is a good arena but the pavilion, though an excellent amenity, is a little too distant from the action to be ideal.

BELPER

Christchurch Meadows, Oberon, Strutt School, Belper Manor, Silkolene, Whitemoor, Belper School

Belper C.C., formed in 1857, lost their ground on Derwent Street in 1879. The Strutt family allowed the club to be reformed on their private ground situated on Christchurch Meadows. With the move came a change of name to reflect their new surroundings and Belper Meadows C.C. first played on their current ground in 1881. To reach the ground one must pass over a cobbled area off Bridge Street. This road leads past the football ground into a car park and the cricket ground is next to tennis courts, a bowling green and an artificial hockey pitch (the hockey club used to play on the outfield of the cricket ground). Apart from a steep bank up to the changing rooms and clubhouse, this is a completely flat and immaculately maintained surface with long boundaries on all sides. The practice nets are situated near the hockey pitch on the far side. A magnificent modern clubhouse raised on columns with a garage below is linked by a corridor to capacious changing rooms. Here we must gripe that the architect did not allow for windows looking out onto the ground. This causes two problems; the players cannot watch the game from the dressing room; and the plain brick wall is ugly. Next to the main building is a large scorebox and shed. Trees and a bank happily obscure the Thornton's chocolate factory next to the ground and the metal railings on this boundary are at least in good condition. The boundary opposite the pavilion is open apart from a few Lime Trees and the next field is a flood plain for the River Derwent that lies beyond. Derbyshire 2nd XI played a number of games on this ground during the immediate post-war years and they returned on a regular basis in the 1990's.

The next field along the river is the well-maintained Thornton's sports ground with two football pitches which in turn leads onto the former ground of Belper Oberon C.C. Oberon were the works team of the George Brettles company. Their ground was established in 1919 and catered for cricket, tennis, bowls, hockey and athletics. Vehicular access was via Chapel Street. Regrettably, it is now a barren overgrown field with no trace of the former pavilion. Strutt School used the ground after Belper Oberon were ejected.

The old school cricket ground in the next field is now the home of Belper Rugby Club. The school was opened in 1909 and their purpose built playing field dates back to this era. Aside from schools cricket, this tiny ground was used by the Spotted Cow team from Holbrook in the early 1990's. The attractive little cricket pavilion has now been extended into an ugly but usefully larger clubhouse by the rugby club.

Another pub team, Welcome Tavern, played Sunday friendlies in the 1980's and used Belper Manor as their home venue. This ground was previously used by the now demolished Parks School until the 1970's. The ground, hemmed in with trees and houses, was long and narrow. This was the ground of Belper Manor C.C., until the advent of the Second World War and their wooden pavilion was opened by the old Derbyshire stalwart L.G.Wright in May 1937. Both pavilion and club are gone and mostly forgotten and the area is unkempt and criss-crossed by footpaths mainly favoured by dog walkers.

The Silkolene Company had a cricket ground at the Gibfield Lane end of their premises in the 1950's. Silkolene were taken over by Fuchs Lubricants who have now sold the entire site for development.

Whitemoor was once the home of Openwoodgate C.C., a leading team in Derbyshire cricket through the 1950's. The club did not stand the test of time and their ground is now used only for 3rd and 4th XI cricket. The changing rooms overlook the two bowling greens, the second of which cuts into the outfield of the cricket pitch to such an extent that the edge of the square is only 25 yards from the boundary at the shortest point. Yet the straight boundaries are among the biggest in the county. The two football pitches are angled to allow a triangular area in between for the cricket square. The outfield is level but very bumpy. The ground is almost totally surrounded by housing but that is partly mitigated by the size of the playing surface. Lacking adjacent facilities and, more importantly, a home club to lavish care and attention on the outfield and square, it is likely that cricket will remain a low priority on this council maintained ground.

Keen eyed cricketers playing on Whitemoor may glimpse the playing fields of Belper School. An artificial playing surface is situated in the middle of a large expanse of mainly football pitches. The portakabins close to the playing fields are not changing rooms – they are situated in the main body of the school – but auxiliary classrooms. The school and playing fields date back to 1974 and were briefly used for senior cricket by the Stevensons Dye Works team.

BIRCH VALE

Hayfield Road

The ground of Birch Vale and Thornsett C.C. is in a field off Hayfield Road almost opposite the Vine Tavern. The ground, established in the first decade of the twentieth century, is surrounded on all four sides by agricultural land and is bordered by a mesh fence. There is a large, modern, brick pavilion at the top of the ground with gravelled ground and seats in between the pavilion and the grass. A new scorebox is in the corner to the right of the pavilion. The playing area slopes downwards with a very sharp incline to the square and another sharp incline after the square. The ground is small and almost completely exposed to the elements.

BIRCHOVER

Recreation Ground, Flower Show Field

Birchover once had two different grounds that were used for cricket. The Recreation Ground off Uppertown Lane was the principal venue for sport in the village and was established in the 1920's. This is still a recreation ground with a modern brick building in the top South East corner that replaced the wooden shed used when cricket was played here. There is a children's playground in the bottom North East corner. The ground has a daunting slope from top to bottom and huge dips on one side. The cricketers abandoned this ground in 1948 and fleetingly played on the Flower Show Field behind Bradley Hall. This is a rough sloping field with an irregular shape and is now occupied by cattle. It was a primitive cricket ground but, with open fields on three sides, the views are pleasant.

BLACKWELL

Miners Welfare

The late Victorian ground of Blackwell M.W. is situated on the prettily named Primrose Hill but this is very much an urban pit setting. Derbyshire played seven first class games here between 1909 and 1913 (J.T.Todd, the colliery manager, was on the Derbyshire Committee) and a world record was set here in 1910 that stands to this day. John Chapman, the Derbyshire skipper, and Arnold Warren shared a partnership of 283 runs in only 175 minutes for the ninth wicket. County cricketers would undoubtedly be horrified if asked to play on this ground today. The football pitch accounts for the majority of the playing area and the cricket boundary is as far across as the centre circle. The straight boundaries are much longer than the square boundaries. There is also a mini football pitch on the cricket side of the ground. The ground is completely encircled by a high brick wall and spectators enter through a turnstile on the football side. The pavilion is on the cricket side and is constructed of the same whitewashed brick as the wall. Indeed, it almost seems to meld into the wall. The 'van body' motor shed and a derelict portakabin do not help the appearance of the ground.

BOLSOVER

Villas Road, Coalite

Bolsover cricket ground is off Villas Road in New Bolsover. The colliery cricket club was formed in 1893 and it reasonable to suppose that the ground dates from this vintage. There are contrasting views from the attractive timber pavilion (c.1913) of the Norman castle high on the hill and a row of well-preserved Victorian terraced housing. The ground is a small plateau with slight slopes on the exiguous straight boundaries. There are white posts all around the perimeter but they no longer have a bar to form a fence. The sightscreen runs along a miniature train line on the Northern boundary. At one end of the square is half an artificial wicket, obviously used for practice sessions or one-sided games. During the 1930's, pit pony races were held on the ground. Derbyshire 2nd XI played here once (against Nottinghamshire in 1974).

The Coalite Ground on Moor Lane is probably a better venue but the cricket ground has to share the turf with football. The grass is well maintained and not significantly damaged by the footballers. Neat high hedges bound most of the ground but housing is visible on two sides. The Coalite Sports & Social Club, a wooden structure painted pale blue, is ugly but practical and a new brick scorebox is planned.

BONSALL

The Park

The Park at Bonsall is a compact playing field near the Forth Memorial. The original size of the field was small when used for occasional games of village cricket but inroads have been made into the grassed area by a childrens playground and a bus shelter. We do not believe that cricket has been played here since the 1960's and it was the narrowest ground ever played upon in Derbyshire. The boundary curves around the road on one side with a stone wall meeting the banked boundaries. The remaining boundary is a heavily wooded steep slope. The house closest to the field was once the Fountain Inn and was used by the cricketers for changing, teas and after match entertainment. The concrete of the practice net is still in one corner and a large modern blackboard with a basketball hoop on the top has stumps painted in white to encourage young villagers to take up the game. If they do, they won't be playing it on this ground.

BORROWASH

G.I.C.

The G.I.C (General Industrial Cleaners) ground at Borrowash off Draycott Road was obliterated by a housing estate in the late 1980's (the Borrowash club last played on the ground in 1987). No trace remains of the ground but the pavilion was at the junction of what is now Appian Close and Roman Way. The southern boundary ran along the disused Derby Canal. The factory of the company closed in 1990 and was demolished in 1994. This was a fine ground and was often used by the Derby & District Cricket Association and the Derbyshire Club & Ground XI. Derbyshire 2nd XI played here once in 1959 against Pakistan Eaglets. The pavilion was a splendid 1912 railway coach and Redrow Homes, who developed the ground for housing, presented it to the Lancashire & Yorkshire Railway Trust. It is currently used by the Keighley & Worth Valley Railway.

BRAILSFORD

Pools Head, Hall Lane

Brailsford and Ednaston C.C. once played at Sundial Farm which is now the village playing field but moved to a new ground

at Pools Head Farm after the Second World War. The old Pools Head ground was extremely primitive. Farm animals had to be removed before start of play and only the square was mown. Teas were served on trestle tables in the open air. The club moved across the road to their present ground in the late 1950's and the old square is now submerged underneath silage pits.
The current ground has evolved into a far superior model than its predecessor. The pavilion is a wooden structure in front of the car park with four supplementary buildings alongside. The scorebox is incorporated into the main building but the players change in one of the smaller structures. Looking out from the pavilion, the ground has a severe slope from left to right with a small bank leading up to a high hedge at the top. The far boundary is fenced and to the right, the ground backs onto one of the greens of the local golf course. There is an artificial net near the car park and an artificial strip on the square.

BREADSALL

Brookside Road, Dam Field, Gipsy Lane

Breadsall C.C. have played on a number of grounds in the village but at one point were obliged to play on the public pitches at the Racecourse in Derby. The current ground, opened in 1968, is situated above Brookside Road next to the school and the views of the church and surrounding area are attractive. The playing area is level and of reasonable size but the football pitch that forms part of the outfield at the top of the ground inevitably affects the condition of the turf. The ground is let down by the pavilion - a flat-roofed monstrosity. The scorebox and motor shed next to the pavilion are even worse.
Before their sojourn on the public parks in Derby, Breadsall used two grounds within the boundaries of the village. Dam Field was used immediately after the war and was part of Church Farm. It is a large field bordered by Dam Brook and the middle part is a raised plateau that formed the cricket square. To the East of the ground is the thunderous noise of the A38 and to the West is the peaceful vista of the village with the church spire poking through the trees.
Dam Field was abandoned in 1947 and for three years the club moved to a ground off Gipsy Lane. Dam Field was terribly prone

to flooding and the new ground was even worse. This field can be seen from the A38 and is sandwiched between the Derwent and the railway line. A broad outline of the playing area can be discerned by the positions of existing trees.

BREASTON

Soldiers & Sailors Sports Club, Holton's Field, Fields Farm, Western Mere Comprehensive School

Breaston cricket ground, on the outskirts of the town, is owned by the Soldiers & Sailors Club in the town centre. The football club has two pitches either side of the square and rent the ground to Breaston C.C. in summer. The ground is too open for comfort with flat fields on three sides and the main road on the other boundary. The ever-present roar of the A52 is audible in the background. The pavilion is an uninspiring flat roofed structure but it is in front of the cricket pitch rather than either of the football pitches. All that remains of the practice facility is a strip of concrete in a corner of the ground.

Breaston C.C. played on West Park in Long Eaton after the War but moved to Holton's Field close to Harriman's Drive in 1954. The following season they moved to a field belonging to Fields Farm. This is now an agricultural field next to a riding school on the North side of Sawley Lane. The pavilion, now an equipment shed on the current ground, was situated in the North East corner of the ground. The farm was sold in the early 1960's and, after a brief return to West Park, the club settled at their current ground.

Western Mere Comprehensive School was opened in 1958 and they had extensive playing fields with six concrete practice pitches. The school was closed in 1990 and completely demolished. The land is currently in a state of flux and the old sports fields are used for horse stabling. The concrete nets are still visible. The ground was used on a regular basis in the mid-1980's by the Pauls Sports & Social Club and occasionally by St Lukes & St Michaels C.C. when the County Ground was unavailable.

BRIMINGTON

Brimington Common, Colliery Ground, Boys School

Brimington, with a population in excess of 8,500 people, is now the largest community in Derbyshire to have no cricket club but three grounds have been used since 1945. Brimington Common sports ground on Manor Road juxtaposes town and country. This is an old venue created out of the Enclosure Act of 1853 (it was certainly in use as a recreation ground in 1877). The field itself is a curious shape; much longer along Recreation Road and the football pitch is tilted across the short side, probably as a consequence of the cricket square that is no longer there. The pavilion, defaced by graffiti, is a double fronted boomerang shaped building with bricked-up windows. There are houses on two sides but there are attractive views looking away from the main road. The Miners Arms, opposite the ground, was handily placed for after-match entertainment.

The Miners Welfare Ground was opened between the wars. It was a substantial facility but eventually succumbed as the collieries declined. It is now underneath Manor Drive and Broom Gardens and the bowling green is the only surviving relic of the sporting complex.

The Brimington Boys School ground was used by Brimington C.C. for their 3rd XI games in the 1980's. The sports field, dominated by the ubiquitous football goalposts, is flanked on one side by the school and falls away to open countryside beyond the ugly metalwork fencing on the other side.

BURBAGE

Green Lane

Burbage Cricket Ground was off Green Lane on the opposite side of the road to what is now Buxton Community School. The small but relatively even playing surface is surrounded by dry stone walls that are now in a state of disrepair. From the road end there are picturesque views of the wooded hills behind the ground. The pitch is currently used by Burbage United Junior Football Club and they have a featureless, windowless, flat roofed changing room building near the entrance of the ground in the South East corner. The old wooden cricket pavilion was in the North East corner.

BURNASTON

Airport

Derby Airport was opened in 1938 and the Air Schools team played on part of the airfield in front of the largest hanger in the immediate post-war years. This area is now underneath the main office block of the Toyota car manufacturing plant.

BUXTON

The Park, Buxton College, Harper Hill College, Fairfield

Established in 1853, The Park is one of the best grounds in the county. The ground is situated on Park Road and was used by the county club on a regular basis from 1923 to 1986. This was the highest first class ground in the country and achieved national notoriety in 1975 when snow stopped play in June. Despite the demotion from first class status the turf is still in excellent condition and forms an expansive and completely level outfield. The current, rather shabby and lacklustre, pavilion with a separate scorebox alongside is on a bank looking over the middle of the square but the traditional wooden structure that preceded this building still stands in the corner by the car park. There is an artificial strip on the square. Although this is very much a town ground, the houses closest to the ground are unobtrusive. The seated area in front and to the side of the pavilion, looks over the playing surface to trees on the opposite side of the ground. A fine ground worthy of an attractive town.

A group of former pupils from Buxton College played in the Buxton & District League after the war as Old Buxtonians C.C. Their home games were played on the College playing fields on Green Lane. The playing fields were probably established when the College was re-opened in 1881 (it had closed in 1817). They were extended in 1892 and leveled between 1895 and 1900. The original pavilion was constructed in 1898 and was paid for by Mr Bingham, described as a 'Manchester businessman' in the history of the school.

The playing fields of the High Peak College at Harper Hill are irregularly shaped with a sharp incline from top to bottom but the playing area is large. Although some of the boundaries are dry stone walls it is not really an attractive ground because it is open and surrounded by a main road, railway lines and housing.

The small, wooden pavilion at the top of the ground is almost completely derelict. The square has disappeared but there is an artificial strip in the centre of the field.
The old village of Fairfield became a suburb of Buxton in the early years of the twentieth century. There was a cricket ground off Tongue Lane that was used by railway teams before the Second World War. After the War it was briefly used by Buxton Co-op C.C. and the North Western Car Company C.C. for matches in the Buxton & District League. The field was owned by the Latham farming family and was eventually sold along with the rest of the farm to become part of the housing estate on the western side of Tongue Lane.

BUXWORTH

Western Lane

Buxworth cricket ground is very small with a steep slope down from the Western Lane side. Over the boundary this slope descends into a sharp drop to the by-pass road and canal. Cricket balls must continually menace the houses on Western Lane and it is a brave man who parks his car next to the ground. The pavilion was opened by Alan 'Bud' Hill, undoubtedly Buxworth's greatest son, in 1997 and is on the top right hand side of the ground. A small scorebox is in the left-hand top corner. There are seats along the boundary to the right of the pavilion. A dry stone wall divides the cricket ground from the football ground next door.

CALOW

Miners Welfare Ground, Civil Service Ground

The Calow Miners Welfare ground is found at the bottom of Oaks Farm Lane, a road that is not recommended for cars of nervous disposition. Once there, this is a good rural ground even though the square boundaries are rather short and a telephone pole spoils the country view. The ground is shared with football with no dividing wall between the two sports but they do not encroach onto each other. The cricket club has a small brick pavilion (erected in 1994) for their own use. The car park is at the football end of the ground.

The Civil Service Ground in Calow is behind Duckmanton Lodge. The cricket field is part of a large sporting complex owned and maintained by the Civil Service Sports Association. In addition to the cricket area, there are tennis courts, two football pitches and a bowling green (an archery club also uses the top football pitch). The cricket pitch is furthest away from the Lodge and slopes down and across. Most of the outfield on one side forms part of a football pitch. The square is angled across in comparison to the football pitches with an artificial strip on the far end. There is a delightful wooden pavilion but the cricketers change in the modern facilities afforded by the main building. The cricket pitch is hedged on three sides with views of the countryside beyond.

CALVER

Calver Sough Park

This is a poor ground with little to recommend it beyond a proximity to the village pub and a neat stone wall that runs round three boundaries. The raised timber pavilion is wholly inadequate for modern purposes without the saving grace of pastoral charm. The square boundaries are the shortest in Derbyshire. A grim wire fence has been erected, presumably to protect the modern housing that has been built around the ground. The ground was first used for club cricket in 1870 but the men of Calver had been playing the game for many years. When Princess Victoria visited Chatsworth in 1832, she watched a game between the estate gardeners and Calver (who won by three runs).

CARSINGTON

Carsington & Hopton Playing Field

The tiny ground at Carsington is owned by the village school but we understand that occasional matches have been played here between local villages. None of the boundaries venture far beyond 30 yards and the total area must make this the smallest senior cricket ground in Derbyshire. The quaint wooden pavilion was funded by the water authority, presumably as a guilty apology for flooding most of the adjacent countryside underneath the reservoir. The outfield is undulating and mole infested but traces of the cricket square endure.

CASTLETON

Hollowford Road, Foxhill

Cricket was played on the Hollowford Road sports ground until the 1960's but this is now the home of Hope Valley Rugby Football Club. There is also a football pitch next to the rugby pitch. Castleton C.C. had moved to this ground in 1948 having previously played on Foxhill behind the main village car park. This is now an agricultural field.

CHAPEL-EN-LE-FRITH

Willow Drive

Chapel-en-le-Frith is probably one of the three best cricket grounds in the Peak District (Buxton C.C. and Glossop C.C. have the others). The club moved to their present ground in 1884 and built a new brick pavilion in 1936. This building was considerably increased in size to a superb modern facility with a spacious bar on the ground floor and changing rooms upstairs leading out to a balcony. The extension was opened by Richie Benaud in 1991. The raised scorebox is flanked on either side by motor sheds and there are two artificial nets next to the right of the scorebox. The ground is not particularly large and there is a sharp dip from the pavilion corner of the ground onto the square but the turf is in excellent condition. Although the ground is surrounded by housing on three sides this is offset by the superb views of the peaks in the background. The town band has their headquarters behind the pavilion. Relations with the adjacent football club, who own the loose stone road to the cricket ground, are somewhat frosty.

CHARLESWORTH

Bankfield

Charlesworth cricket ground is found up a tree-lined path off Marple Road. The ground is known as Bankfield and has been used by Charlesworth & Chisworth C.C. since 1906 (the club predates the ground by around forty years). The ground was rented from Lord Howard who auctioned his estate in the 1920's. The ground was offered to the club for £120. This sum was raised in less than a week and, as a tribute to the local fundraisers, the ground was handed over for £100. Leading on from the drive, a path encircles the ground to the pavilion on the far side. The current pavilion was opened by Colonel Peter Hilton, the Lord Lieutenant of Derbyshire, in 1989 and is two separate buildings with a raised scorebox and balcony atop one part. The ground is distinguished by a tremendous new practice facility next to the pavilion comprising two full-length artificial surfaces with concrete run-ups. The playing area is shaped into a perfect oval.

CHATSWORTH

Chatsworth Park

Chatsworth is a grand estate and the cricket ground is appropriately agreeable. The playing area is extensive though not vast. The delightful timber pavilion with a thatched roof is framed by trees and the boundary to the right is lined with poplar trees with the River Derwent behind. A public footpath that leads to the superb house forms the left-hand boundary. There is a concrete net surface to the left of the pavilion. The current ground and pavilion were constructed around the First World War. The 9th Duke of Devonshire, a keen cricketer, was dissatisfied with the playing surface on the original ground near Queen Mary's Bower that was certainly in use by the early nineteenth century.

CHELMORTON

Main Street

Chelmorton cricket ground was behind the Primitive Methodist chapel field (the chapel has now been converted into a private house). It is a large meadow that drops away markedly after the plateau where cricket was played. There were no permanent buildings constructed on the ground for either changing or machinery.

CHESTERFIELD

Queens Park, Brearley Park, Water Meadows, Chesterfield College of Technology, Tapton House School, Eastwood Park, Hady Hill, Highfield Park, Loundsley Green, Manor Fields, Mullan Park, Sheepbridge Works (Newbold Road), Sheepbridge Works (Sheffield Road), Somersall Playing Fields, Robinsons, Stand Road, Cylinders, Glassworks

Chesterfield lays claim to not only the best cricket ground in Derbyshire but also one of the prettiest venues ever used for first class cricket in the world. Indeed, the authoritative 'World of Cricket' encyclopedia features a picture of the ground as a frontispiece. Queens Park was built in celebration of Queen Victoria's Golden Jubilee in 1887. The Mayor of Chesterfield, Alderman T.P.Wood proposed that land should be purchased from Mr E.A.J.Maynard (the area was known as Maynard's Meadows). More land in the immediate vicinity was purchased in 1892 and the size of the park was increased again in 1901. The cricket ground was opened in 1894 and the first game was played on May 5th (between Chesterfield and Clay Cross Park). The pavilion was built in the winter of 1897-88 to enable county cricket to be played for the first time on 29th June 1898. Derbyshire controversially abandoned the ground after the 1998 season but the local council still maintains the playing surface to a high standard and Chesterfield C.C. play in the Derbyshire Premier League. The ground is slightly elliptical in shape with a concrete path all around that provides a permanent boundary. The pavilion is constructed from timber and brick but is architecturally unremarkable. There is terracing on either side of the pavilion and a small metal stand on the opposite side of the ground. The scorebox is midway between the pavilion and the metal terracing on the southern boundary. The infamous crooked spire can be seen through the trees from the pavilion. This is a lovely cricket ground in a delightful park. The ground is surrounded by mature trees and the park boating lake and bandstand are close by if the cricket palls. Around the county circuit surely only Worcester rivalled this ground for natural beauty although county players thought little of the facilities.

Old Whittington C.C. play on Brearley Park, a publicly owned ground with two adjacent football pitches, neither of which

encroaches onto the cricket field. The pavilion is a brick built, stone-faced structure built by the council in 1979 to replace the railway carriages that were burnt down. The field is bounded by a wooden fence with a brook and houses alongside one square boundary. The playing area is level although there is a bank on the opposite side to the brook that forms an additional non-playing part of the field. There are two artificial practice strips. Old Whittington moved onto this ground in 1955 after their previous ground, Water Meadows off Whittington Hill, proved too small. It was only used as a cricket ground for two years (1953-54) and this tiny ground is now completely overgrown. A public footpath ran along one boundary and the opposite side was formed by mature trees hiding the River Rother.
The playing fields of Chesterfield College on Langer Lane are no longer used for cricket but the little plateau that was the square is still noticeable between two football pitches. The college was opened in 1967 and, apart from the college team, Clay Cross and Rolls Royce used the cricket facilities in the early 1970's. The ground is long and narrow with undulations and a bank on the roadside boundary. There are houses alongside the length of the ground on the roadside but the views from the pavilion are pleasantly rural. The pavilion is a rather ugly wooden structure and is flanked by a big, old roller on one side and a disused concrete practice strip on the other side.
Tapton House was once the residence of the great railway pioneer George Stephenson. It was given to Chesterfield Corporation in 1925 and became a school in 1931. The grounds were turned into a public park. The school sports field was opened to the West of the house across the railway line. The small wooden pavilion was in the South East corner of the ground. It was briefly used for senior cricket in the 1960's by the S & J Kitchen works team before that company built a factory on top of this lengthy field.
The cricket pavilion at Eastwood Park is a small wooden building on a raised stand pronouncing, amidst the graffiti, that this is the ground of Hasland C.C. who played here for many years. That club is now defunct and Eastwood Park is now used by Spital C.C. who lost their own ground at Hady Hill. Although the ground is bordered by housing and roads on two sides, the area

has an atmosphere, albeit slightly gone to seed, of a traditional English pleasure park. Within the park is a war memorial, two children's play areas, a pond, tennis courts, bowling green, five-a-side football pitch and the imposing Eastwood Memorial Hall. The size of the cricket field is restricted by a circular path on three sides and a hill on the southern boundary. The Memorial Hall was formerly Hasland House and was bought from the trustees of Bernard Lucas by Alderman G.A.Eastwood and presented to the people of Hasland as a memorial to his father, Alderman Edward Eastwood, who was born in the village before it became part of Chesterfield. The park was opened in 1913 and the Mayor of Chesterfield insisted the name be changed from Hasland Park to that of the benefactor. The cricket ground is actually older than the park itself because Hasland Church Institute C.C. had played in the grounds of the house for a number of years.

Spital's previous ground was teetering on the side of Hady Hill. The playing area was small and sloping with a fairly grim pavilion in a tree-lined corner (the club, evolved from the old Spital St Leonards C.C., lost their original wooden pavilion to arsonists prior to their diamond jubilee season in 1973). A tarmac path lined with lampposts has been driven through the ground and the remaining greensward has been converted into a five-a-side football pitch. Aside from the limitations discussed above, the ground was relatively pretty with trees curling around two sides and allotments tucked below the western boundary.

Highfield Park was used until 1991 by the Chesterfield Parish Church team and also by Mothers Pride in the Chesterfield Works League. This is a large windswept open ground and is well named. The whole area is on a slope but it dips alarmingly towards the housing on Chantrey Avenue at the eastern edge. There are two pavilions whose aesthetic appeal varies from vile to tolerable. The ground now encompasses three football pitches and a rugby pitch.

The Loundsley Green estate was built in 1963-64 mainly to accommodate the relocation of the Accountant General's Department (A.G.D.) from London. The cricket pitch was constructed soon after and was ready for use in 1966. The A.G.D. C.C. flourished under the guidance of Barbados-born

C.R.W.Suttle who organised an extensive youth coaching scheme on the estate. Those idealistic early years have passed and the A.G.D. team now plays at the Civil Service ground in Calow. The square is still visible on the field but cricket has now been curtailed. Building work is cutting down the playing area and the ground will only be able to accommodate the football field on the far side from the main road. The pavilion is a typical vandal proof council construction with no windows and absolutely no charm.

Manor Fields have been the subject of controversy in recent years. There are two separate fields divided by trees and Manor C.C. last played on the slightly larger field in 1991. They were formerly school playing fields but were sold as surplus to requirements by Derbyshire County Council in 1998. McLean Homes have applied to build luxury homes on both open spaces but have met with concerted resistance from local residents and Chesterfield and North Derbyshire Friends of the Earth. Both fields are attractive, unspoilt and lined with hedges and trees. Due to the cramped area, close proximity to housing and lack of facilities, cricket is unlikely to be played here again but let us hope that these little places of calm can be preserved as a haven of peace.

Mullan Park was a real curiosity. Peter Mullan was an Irishman who made his fortune manufacturing equipment used for opencast mining. He fell in with a group of cricketers at his local, the Rose & Crown and built them a fine cricket ground from scratch in open countryside to the North West of Chesterfield. The ground was oval shaped with an impressive stone and timber pavilion. It was used by Chesterfield Taverners (Mr Mullan's friends from the pub) until 1987. The field is overgrown and the pavilion has been demolished although the foundations are easily discerned.

The Sheepbridge Coal and Iron Company enjoyed the use of a well-appointed and well-maintained sports ground next to the works on Sheffield Road. The ground was opened in 1864 but was replaced by a new facility at Newbold in 1950. The old ground was initially covered by a new blast furnace and is now under the A61 dual carriageway. The road was driven right through the middle of the ground and absolutely no trace remains.

The new ground cost an estimated £30,000 and the company secretary G.R.Clarke said at the time of construction that they hoped to enrol 90% of the works employees into the sports club. The whole complex is an impressive example of what can be achieved with facilities of this kind. The football pitch is fenced and separate from the large cricket field overlooked by an immaculate bowling green and a floodlit five-a-side football pitch. There are hedges and a row of poplars around the ground and the nearby housing is quite unobtrusive. There are two artificial practice pitches next to the motor shed between the football and cricket pitches. The whole area, including the social club and excellent car park, comprises ten acres.

Chesterfield Barbarians played on Somersall Playing Fields for many years but they have recently abandoned the ground for the undoubtedly superior Robinsons Ground at nearby Walton Dam. Their old ground is wedged between the snaking course of the River Hipper and a housing estate. Its length allows for a cricket field and two lengths of football pitches but is quite narrow. The ground is very uneven, particularly on the river side. The former brick buildings that served as the clubhouse and changing rooms have been replaced with two grotesquely unattractive metal freight containers that hardly compliment the otherwise pleasing qualities of the ground. The playing fields were donated to Chesterfield Council by Robinson & Sons in 1927 as a memorial to two company directors, W.B.Robinson and C.P.Robinson.

The Barbarians current home is just down the river as the crow flies but requires a ten-minute detour by road (if the traffic is not too bad). Ironically, this lovely ground was also connected to the Robinsons Company and is approached off Walton Road via a rising curved road. This was the company sports ground built in 1899. Although the playing area is only moderate in size with slight undulations, the turf is excellent. Sadly, the characterful brick pavilion with a verandah and clock turret was burnt down and has been replaced with portakabins. The row of housing on the southern boundary is protected by a high fence and Walton Dam, to the North, is only separated from the ground by a row of mature trees. To the right of the portakabins is a bowling green and to the left is a brick motor shed and small scorebox. The view looking out from the pavilion is attractive open countryside.

Chesterfield racecourse held annual meetings from 1774 until 1877 but the only reminder that horses ever ran around the playing fields that lie in its stead is the name of the thoroughfare that runs alongside – Stand Road. This long, thin strip of land is overlooked at one end by the Cricketers Inn and at the other by the fire station. On the opposite side to Stand Road, trees do their best to obscure the housing beyond. Ad-hoc race meetings were held until 1924 when the Chesterfield Corporation Act abolished them on the grounds that much of the area had fallen into disuse. At this point the land was converted into a recreation ground and became the home of Chesterfield Congregational C.C. It was also used for many years by the Sunday Eleven of Chesterfield C.C. It is currently used by Richland Wanderers C.C. Football is clearly given preference here with three pitches forcing the cricket square into a rather cramped position at the fire station end of the ground. The square ought to be aligned North-South rather than the traditional East-West as the straight boundaries are very short on one side. The pavilion is a hulking red brick structure next to the road opened in October 1994. Further developments are planned here and cricket is included in the scheme.

The sports ground of Chesterfield Tubeworks, later Chesterfield Cylinders, is an excellent ground with an attractive timber pavilion built in 1952. The works cricket team were forced off the ground by demands for impossibly high rental charges after the 1999 season but football and bowls are still played here. The playing area is large and the turf is still in good condition. Houses have been built behind the ground on the opposite side to the pavilion but most of the views are surprisingly verdant for an essentially urban ground close to the town centre. The loss of this good ground, for the playing of cricket at least, is possibly the most serious in Derbyshire in the last ten years.

Also priced off their longstanding company ground in 1999 were Dema (formerly known as BTH, GTC and GB Glass). Unlike Cylinders pleasant ground away from the factory, Dema's ground was in full view of the works with a good deal of wasteland littered with industrial debris over the metal fencing marking the boundaries. The ground is located well below Sheffield Road but is fairly level apart from some rippling undulations. The outfield was always rather rough but is now completely overgrown. The pavilion is of the old-fashioned timber sort and somewhat ramshackle and small.

CHINLEY

Chinley & Buxworth Centre, The Forge

Chinley C.C. has a full committee of officials and some money in the bank. Unfortunately they do not have a team or a ground. A small band of Chinley cricket enthusiasts have twice tried to establish a club on the vast sports field of the Chinley & Buxworth Centre, latterly in the mid-1990's. Both attempts have been doomed to failure because the square that was laid between two football pitches was unsuitable for the game and other local clubs were reluctant to play upon it. This is a great shame because the field would be one of the biggest grounds in the county with mature trees along one boundary and grass banking around the rest. The entire area is completely level and even.

For a few glorious decades, J.J.Hadfield Ltd provided their workers with one of most advanced facilities in Derbyshire. The ground was opened in 1925. It was a substantial playing area near the works entrance with Blackbrook running behind the pavilion boundary. By the early 1950's, the playing area was eaten away by new office and factory buildings but the stately brick pavilion incorporating changing rooms and a social club with a tiled roof and three decorative turrets is still in situ as the works canteen. The home changing rooms were known as 'The Waldorf' and became a separate dining room for the managerial staff of the company. The ground was known as 'The Forge' because the area was used for this purpose before becoming a paper mill and then a textile company.

CHURCH GRESLEY

Gresley Old Hall

Gresley Old Hall was leased to the Miners Welfare by the N.C.B. who had rescued the house from dereliction. The renovated building re-opened in 1953 complete with huge sports fields set around the house in what used to be, before extensive mining, part of a 600-acre parkland estate. The football ground on the front side of the building still appears to be used but the cricket ground, to the right of the house, is now a mown field with no indications of where the square was. Rooms overlooking the cricket ground still contain forlorn reminders of the game such as an old scoreboard propped against a wall. The Old Hall and grounds are still used by the local community for dances, caged bird shows and whippet racing. The ground was last used by Overseal Phoenix in 1993 although it had previously been home to a variety of colliery and non-colliery teams.

CLAY CROSS

Sharley Park, Clay Cross Works (Biwater)

Both grounds in Clay Cross were built by the all-encompassing Clay Cross Company and cricket flourished under the paternal gaze of the Jackson family, owners of the company, whose most famous member, Captain G.R.Jackson, skippered the county side from 1922 until 1930. The first ground was established on High Flat in 1874 and was renamed Sharley Park in honour of the company manager's gardener, William Sharley. The manager in question, Mr Binns, had allowed the ground to be built on part of his garden. It was acquired by the National Coal Board after the war but the colliery team folded in 1972. The current club called Clay Cross that has played on the ground since 1975 was formerly the works team of Kennings Remoulds. The playing surface is generous but uneven with a particularly large dip in the outfield on the opposite side to the Danesmoor Miners Welfare building. The pavilion, set to the left of the welfare, was opened in 1934. It has brick terracing with rooms underneath and a half-timbered room at the top. The building has been vandalised on a number of occasions and the club plans to replace it with a modern building. The square, which has an artificial strip at one end, is not aligned to either the welfare or the pavilion – very curious. The boundary is banked all the way around and was purposely constructed this way to provide a track for the cycling club that was once based here (a similar example may be found at Glapwell). The current club are now in the process of establishing a second ground on adjacent land in the park.

When the collieries were nationalised, a new ground was built for the non-colliery employees of the vast Clay Cross Company. This ground was opened in 1952 and maintained with weekly contributions from the workforce. The surface is flat and in good condition and the boundaries are fairly even all around. The pavilion and scorebox (a single building with a flat sloping roof) with a seating area alongside is raised above the ground in the corner opposite the main gate. There are houses to the rear of the boundary opposite the road but there has been extensive tree planting on the road boundaries and the ground is entirely fenced. Overlooking the ground is an interesting, hexagonal roofed, former railway building called the Rainbow Café. It was transferred from Ashover for the opening of the ground but the multi-coloured 'rainbow' asbestos roof tiles did not survive the move. It was used as the sports pavilion until the current building was constructed. What remains of the Clay Cross Works company is now owned by Biwater. The works cricket club now obligingly call themselves Biwater but they have still been given notice that the ground is to be sold and the future remains uncertain at best.

CLIFTON

Chapel Lane

Clifton C.C. have been the strongest club in the West of Derbyshire for many years and their ground bears the imprint of this success. It is found along Chapel Lane with a very small car park at the entrance and is blessed with tremendous facilities. There are artificial nets in the left-hand corner and an artificial strip on the bottom edge of the square. The old wooden pavilion, perched at the top right hand pinnacle of the ground was opened in 1907 and is now used as a tea room and bar. In front of this building are picnic tables. These are matched by a small picnic area in the other top corner of the ground – a nice touch this. The new brick pavilion alongside, named for a long-serving member Ken Bridge, houses the changing rooms and is entirely in keeping with the ground. There is a fine scorebox dedicated to the memory of Laurie Melbourne and opened in 1998 by Jim Smith (then manager of Derby County F.C.). After the riches described above it is the duty of an impartial observer to note that the slope on the ground is severe with some undulations though the turf is immaculate. The straight boundaries are also quite short for the class of cricket that is played on the ground. Clifton C.C. were formed in 1867 but did not move to the current ground until the 1880's.

CLOWNE

High Leys Road, Mansfield Road, Villa Park

The small town of Clowne now has one cricket ground but, until recently, it had three. The best and oldest (1878 is the claimed foundation date) of them is owned by Clowne Town C.C. who have recently unveiled an enormous new stone-faced brick pavilion. This is an impressive site although the old pavilion, on the crown of the ground, was in a better location than the new building. The ground, situated on High Leys Road, is surrounded by the gardens of houses that are mostly of recent vintage. The straight boundaries are long and the square boundaries are adequate. This is a well-maintained ground with two artificial practice nets and an artificial strip on the square.

Clowne C.C. used to play on what is now known as the Mansfield Road Sports Complex owned by the North Derbyshire Tertiary College. The former area of the square is naturally the best piece of turf, sandwiched between two football pitches, and is now principally used for football practice. Beyond the boundary opposite the brutal looking changing rooms are some more football pitches. In between the car park and the pavilion is a large tarmac surface with floodlights.

Villa Park on Recreation Close is a football ground and never ought to have been a cricket ground. It is located next to housing for elderly people and, after a few years of being menaced by cricket balls, their complaints drove the cricketers away. The pavilion is built of brick and the windows have been breeze-blocked in. There is also a horrible looking motor shed on the ground. Clowne Phoenix C.C. and Scarcliffe C.C. were the principal teams that played here.

CODNOR

Miners Welfare

The sports ground of Codnor Miners Welfare on Goose Lane must be the worst laid out facility in the county. The ground is extensive yet the position of the changing rooms and bowling green means that fine leg/third man are less than twenty-five yards away from the corner of the square. The straight boundaries are vast but the cricket square is pushed up close to the top of the ground by the football pitch at the bottom of the sloping ground. The concrete net facility is also eccentrically placed on the opposite side of the ground to the grubby changing rooms that are in urgent need of some new paint and the removal of some noxious corrugated metal sheeting. The ground is overlooked by the Miners Welfare building and a good concrete car park. Cricket has been played in Codnor since the mid-nineteenth century but the modern ground only dates back to the establishment of the miner's welfare in 1924. The cricket club have recently announced that they have dropped 'M.W.' from their name.

CRESWELL

Miners Welfare

The old Creswell cricket ground is situated between the model village and the former colliery that built both these fine facilities at the end of the nineteenth century. The housing in the model village seems to be in a mixed condition but the magnificent cricket ground, good enough to host matches for Derbyshire 2nd XI in 1972 and 1973, has been sadly neglected. The ground was a capacious oval with metal fencing all around. It has recently been revived for football but the size and shape of the ground betrays its origins. One bystander watching an unrefined game of football assured us that the old groundsman who tended the cricket pitch is now turning in his grave.

CRICH

Top Doctor

The Top Doctor, formerly the cricket ground of Crich United C.C., with glorious views of the attractive town, is now a lumpy sloping field. The wooden pavilion, transported from the football ground that still exists near the market place, was burnt down many years ago. Cricket ceased in Crich in 1963.

CROMFORD
The Meadows

Once there were two pitches on the meadows but the rugby club has obliterated the square on which Old Bailleans C.C. played. Old Bailleans folded in 1993 but their pitch was used for two further seasons by Wirksworth 3rd XI. The ground is found off Mill Road and a rough hardcore track eventually opens out into a huge expanse of grass. The rough stuff outside the wire fence is used for sheep grazing, car parking and walking dogs and the well-manicured turf inside the fence forms the existing cricket ground (used by Cromford Meadows C.C.) and several rugby pitches. The cricket club and the football club, whose pitch is between the cricket ground and the railway line on the far side, share the shabby but charming wooden pavilion. The defunct pitch was served by the dull rugby club building. To the left of the pavilion is a splendid lime tree and further along this boundary are three sycamores. The views are breathtakingly beautiful and must make this one of the prettiest and oldest (1865) grounds in the county.

CROWDEN
Longdendale

Torside C.C. played on a ground at Longdendale in the 1950's. The ground is now buried beneath the car park of a youth hostel.

CUTTHORPE
Recreation Ground

The village of Cutthorpe acquired their recreation ground through the auspices of the Miners Welfare scheme in 1924 and it cost £98. The ground was levelled after local people had extracted coal from underneath the surface during the great strike of 1926 and it remains an even surface to this day. Cutthorpe C.C. have maintained a tremendous standard of cricket in recent years but when they won the Bassetlaw League the size of the ground prevented their acceptance by the Nottinghamshire Premier League. The extremely short South

East boundary, as little as twenty-five yards at the shortest point, is caused by two factors. The football pitch on the northern half of the ground has pushed the square across towards the car park of the 'Three Merry Lads' public house and the car park itself cuts into the boundary. These problems aside, it is a pleasant ground with appealing views of open countryside on the football boundary. The ageing wooden pavilion is perched on a bank but there are separate changing rooms close to the pub.

DARLEY DALE

Station Road South, Whitworth Institute

Darley Dale C.C. play on an excellent ground off Station Road South. It was formed and levelled in 1863 at a cost of £6 12s. A long car park runs off the main road and is divided from the boundary by a white metal fence. An impressive but neglected scorebox stands in the corner of the ground at the end of the car park and the large but old-fashioned pavilion is in the next corner diagonally opposite the entrance. The pavilion was built in 1904 at a cost of £254. This is a large ground with good turf. It is flat and even apart from an area on the pavilion side that shows signs of subsidence. The ground hosted a televised John Player League game in 1974 and, until quite recently, Darley Dale was a powerful club. This is a ground that deserves top-class local sport and it is to be hoped that the club will restore their team to the higher echelons of league cricket.

The other ground in Darley Dale, now unused, is located behind the Whitworth Institute founded by the great engineer and philanthropist Sir Joseph Whitworth. The grounds of the institute are now known as Whitworth Park and the cricket ground was in the upper part below Sir Joseph's memorial obelisk. The playing area was a flat oval (approximately half as long as it was wide). It is lined with trees and surrounded by a tarmac path. It is presumed that the ground was established shortly after the Institute was built at the end of the nineteenth century.

DENBY

Copper Yard, Ryefields, Street Lane, John Flamstead School

Denby C.C. play on a capacious, perfectly flat oval that was purpose built for the game on land that was formerly spoil heaps for the pit. Named the Copper Yard, it was opened in 1982 after the club had endured three years of exile from the village on a public park in Loscoe. They have a large social club but the changing rooms are cramped and hidden behind the motor shed under the scorebox. The pitch is slightly below the pavilion with a high bank on the boundary to the left but completely open and level to the right (this are is used for youth cricket). The boundary opposite the pavilion has a hedge with a bank behind. There are two artificial practice nets next to the pavilion and an artificial strip on the edge of the square. The ample car parking (tarmac next to the pavilion, grass on top of the big bank) make this an ideal ground for big occasions and the club is always keen to stage such matches. The large spoil heap looming to the right of the pavilion has been dissipated in recent years and the adjacent land is becoming verdant with the passing of the years. A rather unprepossessing vista around the ground is gradually becoming more naturalistic and attractive. The Denby club has four senior sides and numerous youth teams and are close to establishing a second pitch in the field behind the pavilion.

Denby formerly played their cricket at the famous pottery. This ground, called Ryefields, is now submerged beneath two large spoil heaps that were flattened over the playing area. It was last used in 1978 and was located behind the factory.

Street Lane in Denby was site of another cricket ground in this far-flung village. The Street Lane club ceased to exist in 1966 and their ground is now wildly overgrown and indistinguishable from the adjacent fields. It was reached via a lane close to the Durham Ox public house and was a small, sloping, uneven venue with a basic wooden pavilion.

The expansive playing fields of John Flamstead School were used for friendly fixtures by the groundhopping NEMCO club in 1987 and 1988. The main cricket field is the highest of several interconnected fields. It is flat and even with picturesque tree-lined scenery. It is quite surprising that another club has not investigated the possibility of basing a team here but perhaps the drawback would be the hefty walk from the pitch to the school changing rooms. There are six old artificial practice strips behind one of the football pitches.

DERBY

County Ground, Racecourse, Raynesway, Alvaston Park, Darley Abbey (Riverside Meadow, Brackens Lane, Ferrers Way, Ford & Weston), Aitons Welfare, Qualcast, The Meadows, Little Meadows, Cables, Derby Omnibus, Carriage & Wagon, International Combustion, Rolls Royce Welfare, Spondon (Asterdale Leisure Centre, British Celanese, Royal Hill Road), Municipal Sports Ground, Rykneld Park, Markeaton Park, Markeaton Lane End, Hodgkinson Memorial Ground, Darley Playing Fields, Parkers Piece, Normanton Barracks, Central Ordnance Depot, Derby County F.C. Training Ground, Bemrose School, Royal School for the Deaf, Art and Technology College, Bishop Lonsdale College, Pastures Hill Secondary School, Gayton Junior School, Merrill College, Littleover (King George V Playing Fields, Rosehill Methodists, Derby Congs, St Chads, Co-op Welfare), Mickleover (Station Road, Mickleover Playing Fields, British Legion Memorial Ground, Pastures Hospital), Kingsway Hospital, City Hospital, Allestree (Robincroft Road),Chaddesden Park, Chellaston (Snellsmoor Lane), Oakwood, Boulton Lane Camp

The County Ground, situated on the Pentagon traffic island, headquarters of the Derbyshire C.C.C., and now the sole venue for county cricket in Derbyshire, is not popular with county cricketers. They probably dislike the gales that blow across the relatively open spaces, the poor facilities, and the lack of atmosphere – crowds are generally sparse and the Derbyshire membership is easily the lowest on the county circuit. However, land around the ground has been sold to private enterprise and this has the double advantage of raising much needed funds and the large buildings constructed around the ground as a direct consequence of the sale assuage the biting winds. A new building on the site of the recently demolished racing grandstand is under construction that will be a pavilion, changing rooms and indoor nets all combined in one space. It has been designed by Fluid, the same architectural company working on the London bid for the Olympic Games. It will also double as a community sports centre which enabled the county club to receive £2.9m from a government body called 'New Deal in the Community'. If county cricket does have a future in Derbyshire at least it ought to be a more convivial experience for both players and spectators.

The ground is still familiarly known as the 'Racecourse' because it stands on the site of Derby Racecourse, a well-regarded venue that hosted the National Hunt Chase on five occasions. The powerful and prestigious South Derbyshire C.C. lost their ground due to a combination of subsidence and the encroachment of the cattle market. They rented part of the racecourse that is very close to where the wickets are pitched today and played their first game there in 1863. The South Derbyshire C.C. were the founding fathers of the county club and Derbyshire C.C.C. took their bow here in 1871. The cricketers had to move west due to the racecourse being widened and their new pitch was too far from the facilities of the racecourse grandstand so a cricket pavilion was built in 1884 (this was later moved from the West boundary to the North boundary). Around this time, Derby County F.C. were formed as an offshoot of the cricket club. Their pitch behind the cricket pitch was used for the FA Cup Final replay in 1886 (Blackburn Rovers beat West Bromwich Albion 2-0 in the first final to be contested by two professional teams) and England beat Ireland 9-0 there in March 1895. The final race meeting was in August 1939 and Derby City Council, who owned all the land, refused to renew the lease to the company that organised racing in 1942. By 1952, a new square was being prepared in front of the old grandstand. In 1955, the pitch returned to its original location and remains there today. The cricket grandstand was demolished to become part of the outfield and for many years the old racing grandstand was used as a pavilion. The ground was also used by a number of local clubs until they were all banished by the county club. St Lukes & St Michaels C.C. was the last local club to play there and they departed after the 1994 season.

When Derbyshire C.C.C. opened their new pitch in 1955, the eastern swathe of the racetrack had already been in use as council cricket pitches since the early 1950's. In terms of clubs registered with the Derby & District Cricket Association, the peak year was 1960 when seventeen clubs - Arcadians, Avon, Breadsall (the only surviving club today), British Rail Research, Cincinatti, Crewton, Derby Electrics, Derby and Midland Warp Knitting, Derby West Indians, Derby YMCA, Magnet, Parker Foundry Sports, Phoenix, Queens Hall Methodists, Revels, Springvale and Vigilants - listed the Racecourse as their home ground. Incidentally, in the same year another nine clubs – Bemrose, British Rail Erectors, Derby Banks, Derby Borough Police, Leys and Ewarts, Old Bemrosians, St Lukes, St Michaels, St Peters – were sharing the County Ground with Derbyshire. Usage on these windswept pitches with minimal facilities declined and in 1979, the last season they were used, only two clubs, Cobra and Derby Eagles, played on the whole ground. The many pitches are now exclusively used by footballers.

The leading club in Derby is Alvaston & Boulton C.C. They were formed in 1857 but their ground on Raynesway between the extremely busy dual carriageway and the rather more tranquil flow of the Derwent was opened as recently as 1950. The club had lost their old ground opposite Alvaston Picture House along Meadow Lane and had to rely on the hospitality of their opponents after the war. Incredibly, they maintained a full programme of away fixtures for two elevens in the immediate post-war years. The current ground is flat and expansive and the river, obscured by banking, bends around the boundary opposite and to the left of the pavilion. The pavilion is a large brick structure, neither attractive nor excessively ugly, in the North East corner of the ground with a good brick scorebox alongside. This was opened in 1979 after two previous pavilions were burnt down. The car park between the road and the pavilion is large and well maintained. The boundary to the right has a high wire fence protecting the Rolls Royce offices beyond. To the left of the pavilion is a row of delightful beech trees that serve to muffle the sound of the traffic and formerly divided the cricket ground from tennis courts. This is now scrubland and the cricket club has yet to decide what to do with this area. A row of nets (the middle of which is artificial) is placed in the South East corner of the ground. The far side of the ground is used for football and Derby County F.C. has recently used other parts of the outfield for junior training. This ground is already an impressive facility with room for expansion and once the conifers planted along the road grow to maturity this will hopefully quieten the incessant whine of traffic.

The public playing fields at Alvaston Park are dominated by football but there is a cricket square close to Wilmorton College. The dimensions of the pitch are governed by a tarmac path on two sides and by trees along a further boundary. As a consequence the playing area is moderate in size but the views are pleasing thanks to extensive tree planting (there is an enormous holly tree in one corner of the ground). The turf is coarse but the entire playing surface is completely level and even. Unfortunately the changing rooms that serve the entire playing fields are not adjacent to the cricket pitch and this ground is likely to remain a 3rd XI venue. The whole park comprises approximately 25 acres and was opened in 1913.

Darley Abbey Cricket Ground, alongside the banks of the Derwent and close to what remains of the old abbey, is a lovely place. This is a modern success story. Two 'public park' teams (Brackensfield C.C. and Abbey C.C.) pooled their resources and, with a little help from Derby City Council, created a new ground from scratch. The two clubs played against each other in the inaugural match in 1986, merged in 1993 and now call themselves Darley Abbey C.C. The brick pavilion, with a tiled roof and wooden balcony, is restrained by modern standards and gazes out across beautiful meadowland with a wall of trees curling around in the distance. The pitch is marked out in a perfect oval with generous dimensions although the square is tilted at an angle to the pavilion but, curiously, is aligned almost parallel to the riverbank that is partially hidden by trees behind the pavilion. The Church of St Matthew peeps out behind the public car park to the right of the pavilion. A fair criticism of this ground must note that the turf on the outfield is not of the highest standard.

During their inaugural season of 1954, Brackensfield C.C. played on Brackens Lane (hence the name of the club). The ground was built over with housing.

There were two previous grounds in Darley Abbey in a large open area off Ferrers Way. The eastern side was occupied by a playing field to the South and a small, attractive cricket ground with a wooden pavilion in the North. This was bequeathed to Kedleston Street Methodists C.C. by a former member of the club. The cricket club severed their connection with the church in 1972 and moved to the Racecourse. Queens Hall Methodists C.C., who had shared the ground, now became tenants and rented alternative Saturdays to Centurions C.C. Both these clubs abandoned the ground in 1975 in the face of Department of Environment plans for the Queensway dual carriageway.

The western side of this open space was occupied by a works ground used by Cox Bros. and then Ford & Weston. They had a large pavilion and the ground was shared with football and tennis. The ground was eventually acquired by International Combustion C.C. and they played here from 1972 until 1984. Queensway (the A38) was eventually driven through the heart of the Methodists ground but the larger ground was converted into housing (the present Finningley Drive). The housing is built around a circular green situated where the old cricket square used to be.

Derby has lost some good company grounds since the war. The Aitons Welfare sports ground on Raynesway was acquired by Derby County F.C. during their halcyon days in the 1970's and renamed The Ramarena. They developed it into two training pitches and added a sports hall. Their ambitious plans to build a swimming pool near the entrance were never realised after the fall from grace following the Clough and Mackay glory years. This is a high quality facility but the playing of cricket would require the removal of fencing and dugouts between the two football pitches.

The Qualcast ground on Haslam's Lane was a huge facility that showcased the famous lawnmowers produced by the company. Both the football and cricket pitches were completely level and well maintained. Overlooking the pitches, on the cricket side of the ground, was an imposing social club. Derby Rugby Club acquired the ground and have restored this venue to some of its former glory.

Unfortunately the former British Rail ground, in the corner of the River Derwent and the main railway line off Siddals Lane, is completely derelict and overgrown with little chance of rejuvenation. This was a flat, square ground with a wooden pavilion and separate scorebox. The ground was known as The Meadows and was the closest sports field to the city centre. It is also one of the oldest grounds in the city. Derby Midland C.C. were certainly playing there in the early 1850's but it does not appear on an 1839 map of the area. When British Rail was privatised, the cricket club asked for a ten-year lease but they were only offered a one-year lease with a six-month cancellation clause and, combined with a large demand for rent, the club folded at the end of the 1992 season.

To the North of The Meadows, over the railway line, was another cricket ground. This was a long narrow ground also used for football and athletics and was called Little Meadows. The works team of Gee Walker & Slater played on this ground until 1954 and it is now buried beneath the Pentagon traffic island and the Meadows Industrial Estate.

The ground of the Derby Cables Company (now known as Draka) on Alfreton Road was completely obliterated by a large factory in 1964. The company was established in 1929 and the ground was in use immediately after the Second World War.

The ground of the Derby Corporation Omnibus Company on Ascot Drive is now bisected by a new road called Newmarket Drive with industrial units on either side placed on top of what was the outfield.

The huge expanse of the Carriage & Wagon Ground is still there. It is overgrown with hillocks of tufted grass and the only evidence of sport here are the white metal goalposts, flat on the ground, almost submerged beneath the grass. This is still an area of tranquil green surrounded by industrial buildings and railway lines but it is more likely to become a nest of industrial units rather than the fine sports arena it once was. Of the pavilion, nothing remains.

The International Combustion Company ground is now a concrete car park but the wooden pavilion is still there, a rotting edifice overlooking a swathe of concrete rather than a greensward.

The only remaining company facility still in company hands is undoubtedly a splendid example and was always the model for this type of ground. This was only to be expected as it belongs to the most prestigious company – Rolls Royce. There are now only two pitches at the Moor Lane facility. Two further pitches on the rifle range are defunct and the square between the football pitches adjacent to the main cricket pitch has recently been abandoned. The main ground is in excellent condition. Although the square boundaries are modest in length this is countered by the fine turf, completely even surface and well-maintained square. The boundary is banked all around. The imposing sports pavilion with a glass fronted function room stands immediately in front of the pitch. The modern part of the building has been grafted onto the old pavilion and the gable and clock tower of the older part are still visible poking out behind the extension. This building is invariably decorated with floral displays. The second existing pitch is behind the bowling green and tennis courts. This is a large ground with a pretty wooden pavilion. The outfield on one side is shared with a football pitch but the turf is in good condition. There are two artificial practice nets close to the pavilion. This ground has a more enclosed feel because the factory units are quite close on two sides but is by no means unpleasant. The club still enters two teams in the Derbyshire County League but after the war they fielded five Saturday elevens and two Sunday elevens and dominated the local cricket scene. Let us hope that the Rolls Royce facilities continue to prosper and that they are kept in pristine condition for future generations as they have almost become a monument and a memorial for all the other commercial grounds that have disappeared in the county.

The former sports ground of the British Celanese Company is on Borrowash Road, Spondon. The entire complex was opened in 1952 at a cost of £240,000 and comprised five football pitches, three hockey pitches, eight tennis courts, two bowling greens, a running track, ruby pitch and three cricket squares. The company social club is now called the Asterdale and the surviving cricket square is used by St Lukes & St Michaels C.C., refugees from the clearance of the County Ground. The playing field is shared with a rugby pitch and the football pitch of Graham St Prims F.C. The boundary to the right of the clubhouse is cut in at an awkward angle by the high wooden fence delineating the ground of Borrowash Victoria F.C. This

particular part of the former Celanese ground is now owned by the football club whereas the remainder of the ground, including the cricket, is leased from the company that own the Asterdale.
The old Celanese sports ground was on Megaloughton Lane close to the factory. This was built in the 1930's and is now literally submerged beneath a water treatment works owned by Severn Trent Water.
Spondon C.C. have a small uneven ground surrounded by back gardens of houses on three sides and a road with houses behind on the remaining boundary. This has the effect of making the ground rather claustrophobic and the piecemeal look of the fences and walls is rather shabby. The raised wooden pavilion and wooden scorebox are in each corner of the Royal Hill Road boundary. In the opposite corner to the scorebox are artificial nets and there is an artificial strip towards one end of the square. In order to maintain the traditional high standing of the club (due to the short boundaries they are unable to be promoted to the Premier League) this ground is likely to be sold for housing and a new site has already been earmarked.
The former Municipal Sports Ground is now the centrepiece of the Moorways Sports facility. It was opened in 1923 and has been the focus of many fantastical schemes since then (for example, a 75,000 capacity football ground for Derby County after the war). Cricket was last played here in 1965 and it now seems to be settled as an athletics arena with a large main stand and banking for spectators all around. A football pitch has replaced the cricket square within the running track.
Cricket on Rykneld Park off Burton Road is but a distant memory. The park is overlooked by high rise housing and a modern path sweeps down and around the steep drop onto the sports field. There are currently two football pitches at slightly tilted angles. This takes into account the worst of the many undulations but also may indicate the location of the old cricket square in between. There has been extensive tree planting in the vicinity of the ground and modern brick changing room stands at the bottom of the hill. Sinfin Victoria C.C. played here in the early 1950's.
Cricket has survived the test of time in Markeaton Park, probably the most congenial public park in Derby. The former

Markeaton Estate was sold to Derby Borough Council for £18,000 in 1929 (Markeaton Hall had already been bequeathed to the council as a museum or art gallery) and the grounds were officially opened in 1931 by the Duke of Kent, the youngest son of the King. The hall was mistreated by the Ministry of Defence during the war and eventually demolished in 1964. The estate has been maintained and included among the 200 acres (the largest public park in the city) is a pleasant cricket ground close to the car park. The turquoise and white pavilion is a hideous structure given the green and leafy environment in which it stands. Next to the pavilion is a large oak tree and there are poplars well inside the boundary on the pavilion side. The pitch slopes away quite alarmingly beyond the square and the turf is little better than the grass in the rest of the park. Nevertheless this is a delightful location made better by the presence of casual spectators (a rare site on club cricket grounds these days). Perhaps they are there for the pitch and putt next to the cricket ground; or to play football with their little children in the wide open spaces; or for a gentle stroll; but an audience is always welcome, however fleeting their presence. Scarsdale C.C. made the park their home for many years until merger and collapse ensued in the 1990's. Recently, it has become a temporary port of call for 3rd XI's and this means that the ground is maintained to the minimum standards expected of council facilities. More seriously, part of the outfield on the pavilion side was wrecked by a pop concert and the boundaries were reduced on this side to around twenty-five yards from the edge of the square.

Arcadians C.C. played on the Hodgkinson Memorial Ground on Blagreaves Lane behind the Methodist Church. The ground was large and flat and generally kept in good condition. Like Wayfarers, the Arcadians converted an old railway carriage into a pavilion. The council sacrificed most of this ground for new housing in the early 1960's. Part of the original pitch is still a small recreation ground but the lower part of the cricket field is now underneath Gary Close.

The Wayfarers ground at Markeaton Lane End was an oval shaped pitch in a long narrow field. This was a notoriously boggy ground, effectively in the flood plain of Markeaton Brook, with a railway carriage pavilion in the corner of the field nearest the headquarters of Derby Rugby Club at the North end. The only evidence of cricket in this field is a concrete practice strip half-buried by grass and hedgerow and a kink in the line of the hedge indicating the curve of the cricket field.

With the demise of all the pitches on the Racecourse, the largest public sports facility in the city is Darley Playing Fields. The whole area comprising around 48 acres is split in two by an avenue of trees. On the Derwent side, there are two squares with very short straight boundaries. This area is exclusively for cricket and can be pleasurable in good weather. The larger side of the field is shared with football. There are currently seven squares but boundaries are a moveable feast determined by the hirer on the day of the match. The outfield on both sides is no better or worse than public facilities anywhere in the county. The changing rooms are a long way from the pitches, there are no scoreboxes and no shelters and the wind blows a cold chill across the open plains. League cricket is not played on these pitches but they are utilised for evening cricket and 'friendly' matches at weekends. Darley Playing Fields, along with Darley Park over the river, were opened on the same day as Markeaton Park in 1931.

Close by Darley Playing Fields in Little Chester is Parker's Piece. This ground on City Road is wedged between the road and the old railway embankment behind the pavilion. It was once ploughland owned by Joseph Parker, purchased and converted to playing fields by Derby School in the 1860's. It was also used by the Derby Town club around this time. After Derby School moved across the city in the 1930's, the ground was taken over by the council. The cricket square is bordered by football pitches on two sides and the outfield suffers as a consequence. This is a large ground that is generally flat and even apart from a small undulating area on the football pitch nearest the main road. It would be almost square but for a large chunk scythed off one corner. The pavilion is a wooden half-timbered construction with a nice gable on the roof. When the foundations for this building were dug in 1925, extensive roman ruins were discovered and excavated. The Derwent runs alongside the boundary opposite the pavilion but is obscured by trees. In recent years the successful Old Derbeians club have shared the ground with

Derby Women. This could be a good venue for cricket, close to the city centre, with an unusual and not unattractive mix of town and country views but it is undermined by the heavy demands of football.

Whither cricket in Sinfin? The Normanton Barracks near the junction of Sinfin Lane and Osmaston Park Road were opened in 1877 and the Sherwood Foresters regiment was based there. There was a well-maintained ground with good facilities opened in 1929 at a cost of over £2,000 (mainly spent on levelling the ground and planting trees around the perimeter). The pavilion was an old-fashioned wooden structure with a verandah built at the same time as the ground at a cost of £264. The last club side to play here were Redfern Athletic in 1980 but Crewton played high-quality local cricket on the ground in the 1970's. The whole barracks was demolished in 1982 and the area is now a cinema complex and other modern units.

Further down Sinfin Lane, on the opposite side of the road to the barracks, the Central Ordnance Depot was a fine ground. This was an industrial area requisitioned by the army in 1938. Surrounded on three sides by mature trees, the turf was immaculate and the pavilion was a good-looking wooden building. This was officially opened on April 26th 1947 when the civilian team played the military team. A variety of governmental department teams played on the ground but when it was last used in the late 1960's, Derby Borough Special Constabulary C.C. was the home side. A factory now occupies the greater part of the ground.

Almost next door to the Depot was the training ground of Derby County F.C., which they also used for cricket, before they moved onto the Aitons Welfare Ground on Raynesway. The ground was behind the County Hotel but the facilities were astonishingly spartan given that it was still used during the highly successful Brian Clough era. Like all the other Sinfin grounds, it has now been built over with industrial units. Just across Shakespeare Street, the recreation ground next to Sinfin Primary School had a small square but was never used by adult sides on a regular basis.

Many clubs in Derby have played their cricket on the grounds of educational establishments. The Bemrose School cricket pitch was used by the Derby Municipal Officers team. The sports field actually predates the building of the school. The old Municipal School was based at Temple House but purchased the grounds of Elm Tree House in 1923 and utilised them as a sports field from 1924. The ground was properly levelled around the time that the new school was constructed in 1930. The new school was named after H.H.Bemrose, a local businessman, who devoted much of his time to education matters in the city. Interestingly, the Old Bemrosians C.C. did not use the school ground as they obtained a pitch on the County Ground.

The Royal School for the Deaf was opened in 1873. Their sports field is behind the school buildings and was built in 1908. It is a spacious area and mature trees protect the ground from the worst irritation of traffic noise from the Markeaton island. Apart from the pupils of the school, the ground was used in the 1950's for inter-departmental matches by British Rail employees.

The Derby College of Art & Technology fielded a senior team in local cricket based on the college playing field on Kedleston Road. The ground was also used by Municipal Officers C.C. The College is now part of the University of Derby and their playing fields, one below the other on the drive up to the main entrance building, are still used by students today (though not for cricket). The top field is a rugby pitch surrounded by a circular cinder track. The larger field below, where cricket was played until 1988, is now divided between rugby and football pitches.

Bishop Lonsdale College in Mickleover has also been incorporated into the University of Derby. This institution was established in 1961 as an offshoot of the Derby Diocesan Training College. The college enjoyed a high reputation for the teaching of physical education and the sports grounds of this institution, opened in 1963, are far more expansive than the Art & Technology College. Two large playing fields are split by banking and trees. There are two football pitches on the far ground and, nearer the college buildings, are three football pitches and a hockey pitch. Cricket nets remain beside the football pitch that runs parallel with the lone hockey pitch and this was where cricket was played by the college team and, until 1989, by International Combustion C.C. This is a rather bleak and open location for sport and changing rooms are too far away from the pitches for comfort.

In the mid 1950's, the County Offices Staff played cricket at Pastures Hill Secondary Modern School at Littleover (now Littleover Comprehensive School). The playing field is a triangular area below the school entrance. There is one artificial strip in the middle of the field with some older concrete practice strips at the apex of the ground furthest away from the school buildings. The school was the first new secondary modern built in the county after the war. The playing fields were seeded in 1951 and first used by the pupils in 1952.

The school pitch of Gayton Junior School has been used more recently. Gayton Community C.C. used the small sloping ground at the back of the school from 1976 until 1986. The ground is square and tightly hemmed in by housing on two sides. A hedge divides the cricket field from another grassed area. The field is still significantly harder in the middle, a legacy of the cricket square. The bottom end of the ground is more uneven than the school end at the top.

Shelton Secondary Modern School was converted into Merrill College and their playing field was used by Lamb Inn C.C. from 1987 to 1991. This was a pub team playing friendly fixtures on Sunday afternoons. The ground is still there on Jubilee Road. It has a single artificial pitch in the middle of the spacious field and six practice strips, now neglected and unused, in a corner of the ground. Metal fences run alongside the road boundary and the opposite side that backs onto waste ground. On the opposite side to the college buildings, a wooden fence separates the ground from the housing beyond.

The district of Littleover was particularly blessed with cricket grounds but they are diminishing with the passing of the years. The main public park is the King George V Playing Fields. This ground was large enough to encompass three separate pitches, but the straight boundaries are quite short for the square in front of the uninspiring brick changing rooms. There have been a number of complaints from adjacent householders in recent years and cricket is not now played in this part of the ground. The middle square has disappeared completely but the remaining pitch is still used by Littleover Centurions C.C. There are two practice nets next to the pavilion and an artificial strip on the disused square. The ground, including a fine timber pavilion, was built at a total cost of £2,250 and was opened by the Duke of Devonshire in 1936. Littleover Parish Council provided the bulk of the costs mainly funded through the sale of other land in the parish. Other significant contributions came from the Carnegie Trust, Derbyshire Playing Fields Association and the King George V Jubilee Fund from which the ground derives its name. The original pavilion was destroyed by fire in 1962 and the current brick building was opened the following year at a cost of £9,000.

Two church grounds are still used off Brayfield Road. The ground of Rosehill Methodists C.C. was opened in 1924 on land donated by a former Mayor of Derby, Alderman A.H.Domleo, as a memorial to the members of the church killed in the war. This ground has a small car park off Littleover Lane. On one side of the car park are the rickety wooden changing rooms and scorebox of the cricket club and on the other side is the bowling club pavilion with the green behind. The turf is unsophisticated and the ground does slope but all the boundaries, especially the straight ones, are adequate in size. There is an artificial practice strip on the outfield at the tennis court end.

The car park of the Derby Congs ground is alongside the North-West corner of the Methodists ground and it is possible to watch the cricket on both grounds with a turn of the head. The facilities on Congs' narrow sloping ground, opened in 1922, are far superior to their next-door neighbour. In addition to the splendid brick pavilion (opened in 1995), the ground has a scorebox, motor shed and two artificial practice nets near the pavilion. Sadly the square boundaries are very short and impossible to alter with housing on both sides and the slope from top to bottom is prodigious.

There were two other grounds alongside Derby Congs that have now disappeared underneath housing. The St Chad's ground was used by Derby Red Rose C.C. until 1973. This was similar in area to the existing grounds but better proportioned. There was a capacious pavilion at the bottom end of the ground with tennis courts alongside. The housing on top of this ground has been given cricket-related street names (Pavilion Road, Trent Bridge Court etc.).

The Co-op Welfare Sports Ground was immediately South of St Chad's and was the first to be sacrificed for housing. A number of Co-op teams played on this ground and the dairy team were the last to do so in 1968. The pavilion was firstly, an old railway carriage and latterly, a plain wooden structure. The East end of the ground was the Co-op bowling green.

Mickleover Sports club have converted fields into two football pitches and a cricket pitch within fifteen years but, in truth, the cricket field is the least hospitable facility on the site at the junction of Station Road and Radbourne Lane. Plans were made in 1986 and by 1991 the lease was agreed and drainage work begun. The ground was opened in October 1992. The cricket pitch has to share the shorter side of its square boundaries with the football pitch and, as a consequence, the turf is fairly rough. During the football season the football pitch is fenced off along the line of the square with floodlight pylons on the outfield (they are removed in summer and the holes covered with boards). The large pavilion with impressive facilities is constructed to overlook the main football pitch and viewing for cricket spectators is limited and uncomfortable in adverse weather conditions. The cricket section has not been completely neglected and they have a double lane artificial turf practice area and a big, traditionally styled, scorebox close to the back of the pavilion. A high hedge protects the Station Road boundary and there is a farm over the far boundary.

Despite the criticism made above, the Sports Club is to be congratulated for their new ground particularly when compared with their former home on the Vicarage Road Playing Fields (known as 'Radford's Pleasance' to locals). This is a narrow yet lengthy field with a heavy slope up from the main road and car park. Two football pitches are still marked out but it may be assumed that cricket will not be played here again. The foundations of the old wooden pavilion, razed to the ground by arsonists, are still evident in the car park and this structure was replaced by an ugly brick council building that is now festooned with graffiti. There is housing on three sides of this ground with a path on two boundaries.

The Mickleover Royal British Legion ground is adjacent to the Legion building on Western Road. The football ground is now surrounded by permanent metal fencing that would make cricket impossible on this rectangular ground (the straight boundaries were quite short). The field is slightly undulating and the football ground is squashed into the far side from the unremarkable Harry Blow pavilion next to the car park. Cricket was last played here in 1997.
Pastures Hospital, a good looking early Victorian asylum, was blessed with a golf course, bowling green, tennis courts, football ground and cricket ground. The hospital has been sympathetically converted into luxurious flats but the cricket ground is now looking shabby and unloved. The ground is behind the hospital with steps leading down a high bank onto the playing surface. There is a quaint wooden pavilion on the far side but the changing rooms were latterly situated over the football pitches near the orangery and church. The straight boundaries are short but the square boundaries somewhat longer. The asylum was opened in 1848 and G.H.Gordon, in his small history, says that "from the very beginning patients enjoyed various forms of entertainment." He adds that cricket was played by the male patients so can we assume that the cricket ground is contemporaneous with the buildings?
The ground at Kingsway Hospital (founded as the Derby Lunatic Asylum in the Victorian era) has not been used as recently as Pastures Hospital; the Kingsway Hospital's cricket team ceased to maintain a regular fixture list in 1988; and the square has disappeared. The lowest part of the ground, nearest the hospital, is undulating. This rises to a plateau in the middle and then falls away to the road. This end of the ground is level. There are a line of trees on one side and the social club (now boarded up) on the other side. The hospital is now closed and the future of the site is uncertain, but the turf is still in good condition and it would be relatively easy to re-establish cricket on this attractive ground.
The City Hospital, off Uttoxeter New Road, has concreted over their cricket ground and it now lies underneath Car Park No.1.
Allestree C.C. once played at Allestree Hall and Clay's Field but have occupied their current attractive ground since 1894. The outfield is in good condition, the pavilion is large but

sympathetically designed next to a wooded bank, there are two artificial practice surfaces in the South-East corner and the ground is on a plateau revealing agreeable views of the village. The straight boundaries are lengthy but the narrow square boundaries are a major drawback. For many years, only straight hits over the boundary counted six (pegs were placed in the corners of the ground to indicate the limits). Unfortunately, the ground cannot be extended without a massive earthmoving operation that would also require either the removal of the woods on the pavilion side or the destruction of the bowls club on the lower side nearest the main road. Neither of these are likely scenarios but thanks to the Gisbourne family, who gifted the land to the people of Allestree as a war memorial, this will remain a fine venue just below the highest standards of local cricket.

Chaddesden Park, opened in 1923 on land gifted by the Sitwell family, is quite a large ground contained within a public park and therein lies the main drawback to playing cricket here. The pavilion is, by necessity, a modern, fortified, council building that is common throughout the county. The ground slopes down from the pavilion with a cafeteria and rangers office to the left and football pitches to the right almost as far into the distance as the eye can see. There are trees on all four boundaries but houses peek through and over the greenery so that it is impossible to forget that this park and cricket ground are surrounded by one of the largest housing estates in the Derby conurbation. The current ground at Chaddesden Park is unlikely to be the same part of the park that was used by the South Derbyshire Club as far back as 1835.

Chellaston has a cricket square squeezed between several football pitches. There is an artificial wicket on the square and the large pavilion is a typically functional but unromantic council ground building. It would be difficult to imagine a club making this ground their own and it is likely to remain a convenient 3rd XI ground for nearby clubs. The ground is reached down a pokey road called Snellsmoor Lane.

Unlike most modern housing estates, Oakwood does possess excellent leisure facilities. Close to the excellent Springfield Leisure Centre is an expansive sports ground with a large pavilion that doubles as a community centre. The pavilion has steps onto the ground and a nice clock tower. Unfortunately for cricketers, the square is wedged between three football pitches, one in front of the pavilion and two on the far side. The entire ground is completely level. When the trees planted around the ground eventually mature they will ameliorate the somewhat bleak and exposed aspect.

Finally, in Derby, a puzzle. The Derby and District Cricket Association handbook of 1949, a wonderful historical record of club cricket, lists a team called British Legion (Allenton). Their ground is given as Boulton Lane Camp. This club does not appear in the 1948 edition and they moved onto the Municipal Sports Ground in 1950. Boulton Lane Camp has long since been built over with housing and we have no idea where the ground was within the camp, nor what it looked like. Are there any cricketers out there who played on this ground?

DOVE HOLES

Halsteads

Dove Holes cricket ground is off Halsteads, the main road through this drab village. It is a workmanlike ground shadowed by a new housing estate, a community centre and a big multi-purpose hard court that is divided from the ground by a dry stone wall. A considerably larger, but not necessarily prettier, stone-faced building has just replaced the shabby, ageing, wooden pavilion. This is on the boundary nearest the main road. A large brick scorebox is on the opposite side of the ground to the pavilion. The ground dates from around the First World War and was rented from the I.C.I Company until 1981 when it was purchased by Dove Holes Community Association.

DOVERIDGE

Sand Lane

Visitors to Doveridge Sports Ground on the corner of Derby Road and Sand Lane would be hard pressed to imagine how cricket was ever played there. The ground is an awkward dogleg shape due to the positioning of the village hall. There are currently two football pitches and a playground. The football club has a modern brick clubhouse in the corner of the ground nearest the roundabout that replaced a pretty, black and white, wooden pavilion. Doveridge C.C. disbanded around 1990.

DRAKELOW
Power Station

The sports ground at Drakelow Power Station was used until very recently by the employees for both football and cricket. The ground is entered by a separate entrance to the station itself and is not inside the boundary of the works. There are substantial brick and metal gates that lead into a spacious car park. The cricket ground is next to the car park and the wooden pavilion and scorebox (both painted white) are in front of the main road. Power lines cut directly above the square across the field and the huge chimneys are directly in front of the view from the pavilion. Every effort has been made to make this ground visually pleasing with plenty of trees and hedges but it is still dominated by its overbearing owner.

DRAYCOTT
Hopwell Road

Cricket was played in Draycott as early as 1849 but the last resting-place for the sport in the village was next to the school on Hopwell Road. This is a public recreation ground used for football and was certainly a tight ground for cricket. After the demise of Draycott C.C. in 1979, the ground was briefly taken up by St Lukes & St Michaels C.C. (1981-83) and Risley C.C. (1984-88).

DRONFIELD, DRONFIELD WOODHOUSE & COAL ASTON
Stonelow Playing Fields, Chequers Ground, Henry Fanshawe School, Stonelow School, Prestwich Sports, Carr Lane, Oxclose Lane (two separate grounds)

There are two cricket pitches next to each other on the Stonelow Playing Fields, separated by a high grass bank and a line of trees. Both were established in the 1960's after the traditional venues in the town were lost to developers. The top ground is used by Coal Aston C.C. and is much the better of the two. This ground is a large oval used exclusively for cricket. They have brick changing rooms next to the car park and a traditional wooden pavilion diagonally across the ground. The outfield is quite spacious, even and in good condition.

The bottom pitch, used by Dronfield Sports, suffers by comparison. The square, in immaculate condition, is uncomfortably angled to accommodate a football pitch and a hockey pitch. Beyond the hockey pitch, is another football pitch and although the boundaries are lined with mature trees, factory units peek through the greenery. Although this is a massive ground, the boundaries of the cricket area are very short on the pavilion side. The pavilion is a converted portakabin spruced up with green paint.

Why then do Dronfield play on an inferior pitch to Coal Aston? Dronfield Sports were formed by members of the Contact Club, which is effectively the Labour Party Social Club. When the Stonelow Playing Fields were established, Dronfield Contact Sports played on the top pitch. After a change in local government they were moved below and the long-established Coal Aston club, who lost their ground in 1965, moved onto the top pitch.

Coal Aston C.C. had played at the small and sloping Chequers Ground. This is now underneath the car park and the 'Wacky Warehouse' extension of the Chequers public house. The open vistas around the ground have been eclipsed by houses and commercial premises.

The old Dronfield Town C.C. played on the Henry Fanshawe Grammar School Ground on Green Lane. This was a splendid facility used for cricket, rugby and hockey with a high stone wall along the entire Green Lane boundary. The pavilion was a handsome wooden structure with a verandah. Old Dronfieldians C.C. also played on this ground. This ground vanished beneath the Greendale Shopping Centre and the Ash Tree public house after the close of the 1968 season.

Coal Aston C.C. has fielded a third eleven in recent years and they play on the capacious sports field of Stonelow School which is separated from the main ground by a wire fence. This ground has the usual strengths and weaknesses of modern school grounds. The playing surface is level with plenty of room and cut on a regular basis but there are no facilities next to the ground and the pitches are not up to the standard of good club tracks.

Almost backing onto Stonelow Playing Fields, is the former cricket ground of William Prestwich and Sons. The ground was opened in the 1930's and the company team became one of the best sides in North Derbyshire after the war. The company developed financial problems and eventually came into the hands of the Padley & Venables company who maintained a cricket team until the early 1980's. The ground is now solely used for football but the curved corners and unused turf on the footpath side of the ground betray its origins as a cricket ground. A dugout has replaced the old wooden pavilion and the concrete strip formerly used for cricket practice is now obscured by grass and weeds. The ground is fenced and lined with trees on three sides and the GPC Derwent factory has been constructed on the other boundary (this was once a factory yard). The Padley & Venables factory is next to the ground on the footpath side.

Dronfield Woodhouse Sports & Social Club have a sports ground on Carr Lane to the West of the town. The cricket pitch is sloping and uneven and a chunk has been taken out of one corner to build a basketball court (former tennis courts). Part of the outfield is used as a junior football pitch. Two boundaries back onto housing although there is a neat hedge at the bottom end of the ground. Next to the small pavilion, painted an ochre shade, is a big sycamore with a seat underneath, a nice touch on an otherwise prosaic ground. The ground was built in the 1920's for the Miners Welfare team. For many years, Dronfield Woodhouse Welfare, playing on the existing ground, maintained a strong local rivalry with Dronfield Woodhouse Sports, who had two different grounds behind Oxclose Lane. Both these grounds succumbed to housing. Both clubs shared the ground until the Welfare club ceased to exist. The council owns the ground but the club owns the pavilion.

DUFFIELD

Eyes Meadow

Duffield C.C. were formed in 1878 and played in the grounds of Duffield Hall, which is now the headquarters of the Derbyshire Building Society. They moved to Eyes Meadow, a large expanse of grassland to the South East of the village, in 1895. The Rolls Royce Company owned the entire meadow until the Parish

Council acquired it in 1974. The ground, close to the confluence of the Derwent and Ecclesbourne rivers, is completely encircled by a fence constructed of concrete and metal. The large, two storey pavilion, almost completely rebuilt after a fire in 1952, is painted white apart from the Claude Lilley Memorial Scorebox next to the balcony that is inevitably painted black. The playing surface is an ample level oval with good turf. A railway line runs parallel to one boundary but the nuisance of noisy trains is ameliorated by mature trees and the road to the ground in between. The opposite boundary has a cluster of large pine trees and agreeable views of Duffield Bank. The spire of St Alkmund's Church may be glimpsed in the view towards Derby and the balcony of the pavilion is a delightful place to wile away an evening after a match. Derbyshire 2nd XI played several limited overs matches on the ground, the first of them being a high-scoring game against Durham in 1996.

ECKINGTON

Renishaw Hall

Eckington Cricket Ground, within sight of Renishaw Hall (seat of the Sitwell family built in 1625), is located in an attractive country setting though the appearance is marred by a large electricity pylon near the entrance with wires running along the length of one boundary. The Sitwell's laid out the ground in 1885 for the use of visitors to the hall and the estate employees. This type of country house cricket died either before or during the First World War. In 1921 Sir George Sitwell offered the ground to the St Peter's church team. This team flourished between the wars but declined in the early 1960's. A team of insurance men called Sheffield Lombards began sharing the ground in 1963. Teams with three different names: Eckington, Eckington St Peter's and Sheffield Lombards played under the aegis of the Renishaw Hall Cricket Association but the march of time has merged them together as Eckington C.C. The ground is approached down the same rustic road that leads to the Hall and one boundary is formed by a substantial stone wall behind which lies the main buildings. The lengthy straight boundaries are almost half as long again as the square boundaries. The outfield is well maintained with good turf but does slope on the scorebox side. The charming old wooden pavilion built after the Lombards moved onto the ground is still standing but has been partially replaced by a new whitewashed brick building decorated with a colourful Sitwell coat of arms. Between the old and new pavilion is a brick motor shed. All these buildings are shaded by a wood directly behind. The wooden scorebox is midway along the boundary between the hall end and the pavilion end.

EDALE

Coopers Cafe

Edale Cricket Ground is now part of Cooper's Camp Site at Grindsbrook Booth. The square was the only level piece of ground and this is now the site of the camp standpipe. The considerable slope meant that the wickets were pitched across the field and the straight boundaries were miniscule because the field is less than seventy yards wide. There is a dry stone wall along the left-hand boundary and a brook running all the way down the right hand boundary. The cricket club used to change in an old tramcar that was placed in the top left-hand corner. When it was used as a cricket ground it also doubled as a cow field during the rest of the week leaving obvious hazards for the fielding side on match days. Cricket was first played in Edale in the 1880's and a picture exists of the 1905 XI on this ground. The club disbanded in 1959.

EGGINTON

Park Hall

Park Hall on Hilton Road was once owned by British Boys for British Farms, an offshoot of the Y.M.C.A. formed in 1932 to promote agricultural careers for young men. They played cricket in a field close to the hall in the 1950's. The building is now used by two businesses and the cricket ground is just a rough field.

ELTON

Jubilee Playing Field

The Jubilee Playing Field is prominently placed in the village on Main Road. The field was a meadow used for various sporting activities since at least the 1920's (older members of the community still call it the 'cricket field') but was purchased by

PLATE 1 - ELYSIAN FIELDS (1)

(Above) The Rutland Recreation Ground at Bakewell opened in 1880
(Below) Parson's Croft at Parwich, happily restored for cricket in 1994

PLATE 2 - ELYSIAN FIELDS (2)

(Above) The Park at Riddings, established in 1847
(Below) The Field at Shipley, opened in 1899

PLATE 3 - LOST IDYLLS

(Above) Edale CC played in this field until 1958
(Below) The improbable looking ground of Hopton & Carsington CC near Hopton Hall was last played on in 1955

PLATE 4 - INDUSTRIAL DERELICTION

(Above) The Chesterfield Glassworks ground has been unused since 2000

(Below) Opened with high hopes in 1952, the Staveley Works ground is now a golf driving range

PLATE 5 - UNUSUAL GROUNDS

(Above) The ground at Old Glossop is virtually triangular
(Below) Osmaston Polo Ground is vast and the pavilion is a splendid relic of a bygone age

PLATE 6 - INTERESTING PAVILIONS

(Above) One of the few remaining traditional wooden pavilions with a scorebox turret at Matlock
(Left) The art-deco wonder at Hope Cement Works, opened in the 1930's

PLATE 7 - PARAGONS (1)

(Above) The unusual, thatched, cricket pavilion on the outstanding school ground in Derbyshire at Repton
(Below) The Rolls Royce Company built their superb sports ground in the 1920's. It remains the best of its type in the county

PLATE 8 - PARAGONS (2)

West Park at Long Eaton, the best multi-pitch public park facility in the county

the villagers and opened as an 'official' venue in 1977. A committee of trustees runs it on behalf of the people of Elton. There is small drive with scrubland and a chicken coop to the right before stepping onto the football side of the ground. The pavilion is in the North East corner of the ground and is dedicated to Alan 'Satch' Mosley, a former captain of the cricket club. It was formerly used on the Friden Brick Works ground. The scorebox next to the pavilion is an old railway wagon complete with wheels. There is a small playground behind the pavilion and tennis courts in the North West corner. The view over the boundary is magnificent. A curiosity of the playing area is a large tree-stump about twenty-five yards from the edge of the square with a newly planted rowan growing behind the stump. The new tree is going to prove a considerable hazard to the cricketers when it matures. The outfield is rough, undulating and sloping down from the pavilion. At approximately 260 metres above sea level, we believe that this is the highest ground currently in use in the county.

ELVASTON

Elvaston Castle

Elvaston Castle and its grounds, former seat of the Earls of Harrington, was the first council owned Country Park in Great Britain. Within the borders of the park is a wonderful cricket ground. Approaching the ground on the rather rough park road, the first eye catcher is the splendid brick pavilion complete with a balustraded balcony and tiled roof made from antique tiles obtained from a barn. This building replaced an awful flat roofed 1960's building (previous changing rooms on the ground had been a shed and a railway carriage). Behind the pavilion, the perpendicular tower of St Bartholomew's Church can be glimpsed through the massed ranks of trees. The trees continue along the castle boundary with a stone wall marking the boundary. The castle itself cannot be seen from the cricket ground. The road boundary has an ascot rail and the ground is divided from a neighbouring field by a wood and wire fence. The new scorebox and motor shed next to the pavilion is perhaps too plain compared to the splendour of the surroundings but it will be impossible to decorate or obscure the brickwork as the club have inscribed the names of contributors in the bricks. From a cricketing point of view, the pitches are always good and the turf is closely mown. However, the outfield is bumpy especially on the pavilion side and a large tree well within the playing area (around point/mid-on) is quirkily romantic but irksome. Cricket was played in Elvaston as far back as 1849 but no satisfactory dating is available for the current club and ground. The Earl of Harrington sold the entire estate in 1963 and it eventually came into the hands of Derbyshire County Council. The cricket club's lease ran out in 1991. Luckily the publicity that ensued from winning the National Village Championship in 1994 forced the hand of a previously disobliging council and a new, albeit more expensive, lease was agreed.

ETWALL
Church Hill

Etwall Cricket Ground, dating from 1889, is close to the centre of the village on Church Hill. This is a good-looking ground bordered to the South by a brick wall that conceals the church graveyard. The pavilion was clearly constructed in two phases with two pitched roofs connected by a flat roofed passageway. There is an excellent modern scorebox adjacent to the pavilion and two artificial practice nets in the corner of the ground opposite the entrance. The square has an artificial strip on the far end but the ground slopes alarmingly away from here with severe undulations. At the bottom of this slope is a sharp drop to John Port School's extensive playing fields that include an artificial cricket wicket and a very impressive array of practice nets.

EYAM
Hawkhill Road

The Eyam Sports Association caters for football, tennis and cricket on the playing fields and, of the three, cricket is the least suitable for this ground. The football pitch is on a raised plateau to the left of the flat-roofed, stone built pavilion. The tennis courts are in the top right hand corner of the ground. The cricket ground lies between the tennis courts and the car park. A stone wall runs down the right side of the ground and it is painted white to act as a sightscreen where it runs parallel to the square. Below the square, the ground drops sharply with some absurd pits and hollows. The playing area is small and must be a nightmare to field upon.

FLAGG

Mycock Lane

Flagg cricket is fondly remembered by ageing cricket aficionados in North West Derbyshire for the involvement of the Boam family who constituted most of the team. A former member of Old Buxtonians C.C. believes he played against a Flagg team consisting of ten members of this family. To many locals the undulating field opposite the bottle bank on Mycock Lane is still known as the 'cricket field'. The field rises from the main road up to a small plantation of trees. The grass is rough and unkempt but was probably little better when used as a cricket field. The ground was never blessed with any kind of permanent structure for changing rooms.

FRIDEN

Brickworks Ground

Thanks to a cricket-loving manager at the brick works in Friden (now DSF Refractories and Minerals) there was a formidable cricket ground out of all proportion to the needs of the local community. The ground was next to the factory with a row of trees planted to obscure the view of the works and set back from the main road. It had a dry stone wall on three boundaries and a wire fence dividing the cricket ground from the rest of the large field in which it was set. All that remains today is a set of gang mowers rusting and overgrown with grass and a small shed housing a mower, nets and other cricketing paraphernalia. The wooden pavilion was sold to Elton C.C. and is still used on their ground.

GLAPWELL

Park Avenue

Here we have an inspiring example for all colliery grounds no longer supported by the proceeds of the coal mining industry. Park Avenue, opened in 1948, is in excellent condition; there is a new brick pavilion with rendered walls and a tiled roof (opened in 1994); a large painted brick scorebox and two artificial practice nets. The ground has some disparate neighbours; the football ground (now completely fenced off) opposite the pavilion, gardens on one side and a garden centre on the other. Like Sharley Park in Clay Cross, this ground once had a cycle track around the boundary. This is now a useful cinder path. The ground has ample straight boundaries but the square boundaries are modest. The new pavilion is slightly out of synch with the square. The old colliery ground was at Doe Lea in the shadow of the pit head. It was known as The Meadows and opened in 1909. This ground was used up to 1942 when the land was taken for spoil tipping. It is now submerged underneath the new road built to take traffic off Junction 29 of the M1.

GLOSSOP & DISTRICT

North Road, Old Glossop, Co-op Ground, Pyegrove, North Western Road Car Company, Hawkshead, Tenfoot Fields, Gasworks, Dinting (Holy Trinity, Olive & Partington, Dinting Vale), Woods Mill, Brookfield, Maconochies, Field Head

Glossop C.C. moved from their ground on Norfolk Street in 1880. This ground was provided, rent free, by the Duke of Norfolk but was too small and impossible to enclose (admission was charged for matches and the boundary had to be patrolled to prevent spectators avoiding payment). The new ground, on North Road, cost over £1,000 and over half this sum was loaned to the cricket club by the Rev. C.B.Ward. It is entered through an imposing set of gates and unsurprisingly, considering the problem of freeloading spectators on the old ground, is fenced on all four sides. To the left of the large car park is an artificial net and a bowling green. On the right of the car park are the two-storey pavilion and the main bowling green. The pavilion is brick built but not of modern vintage and is slightly small for modern tastes. There is a lawn in front of the pavilion and the right-hand side of the ground has a high fence covered with sponsor's boards with seats in front. On the opposite side is a raised bank for spectators with the railway line behind. The far boundary is a high hedge with a scorebox and motor shed in the right hand corner. The playing surface is flat, lush and large. It is a loss to

Derbyshire cricket that this imposing ground has always belonged to a club that chooses, for understandable geographical reasons, to play in other counties. Sir Samuel Hill-Wood was a great supporter of Glossop C.C. around the turn of the nineteenth century and many county cricketers were enticed to the club by his wealth. He captained Derbyshire between 1899 and 1901 and, thanks to his personal financial guarantees, the county played fifteen first class games on the ground between 1899 and 1910.

The ground of Old Glossop C.C., entered off Manor Park Road, is charmingly unusual. Although club luminaries will blanche at such a description, this is ostensibly, a triangular ground. The longest boundary, with a kink in the middle, is divided from housing on Manor Park Road by a high, whitewashed brick wall and the open boundary to the right of the pavilion has a whitewashed dry stone wall. The ground was constructed in 1901 when four men, bemoaning the lack of cricket in Old Glossop, approached Lord Howard and asked to rent some land. They rented two small fields divided by a stone wall. The wall was demolished and used as ballast to level the square. The club bought the ground from Lord Howard's estate in the mid-1920's. The club chairman, Mr S.T.Ashton, editor of the Glossop Chronicle, raised £60 for the purchase by organising two shows at the Glossop Empire Theatre. The old wooden pavilion (now converted into a scorebox) is perched at the apex of the triangle but the new stone-faced pavilion (c.1992) is in the bottom right-hand corner of the ground. There is an artificial pitch at the bottom of the square and there is a concrete net next to the pavilion. The site of an earlier pavilion and earlier nets are still in evidence on the bottom boundary and the groundsman uses these strips of concrete to service his machinery. It is likely to remain a unique oddity – the only three-sided ground in Derbyshire.

Old Glossop's ground was the first of four grounds in adjacent fields. Next door was the Co-op ground later used by the Vol Crepe Company. Cricket was last played here in 1970, but it remained as a football ground for some years after. In the next field was Pyegrove and, finally, the North Western Road Car Company ground. The Co-op Ground is now wildly overgrown with only rotting football posts to remind visitors that this was a sports field. Pyegrove is a roughly cut recreation ground with a tennis club and a children's playground in opposite corners along the Sheffield Road boundary. The Car Company ground is buried beneath housing.

The Hawkshead Ground on Silk Street was one of the poorer facilities in the town. The outfield was very uneven and the grass was rough. The pavilion was a modest wooden structure. Hawkshead C.C. disbanded in 1968 and the ground is now totally covered by houses.

The Sumner's Mill works team played at Tenfoot Fields off Brook Road but the actual location of the ground is nigh on impossible to ascertain.

The Glossop Gasworks ground is situated on the edge of town opposite the entrance of the cemetery. This may be the ground once used by Glossop Dale C.C., the first club in the town formed in 1833. It is an oval ground big enough to accommodate two football pitches. The cricket square was between the football pitches. The field is below the level of the main road with even larger drops off the other side of the ground. Cricket has not been played here since the 1970's but it survives as a football ground. The brick changing rooms are unsightly.

Holy Trinity Dinting C.C. play on a ground off Simmondley Lane that is still owned by the church (the spire is visible from the ground). There is a new flat roofed brick pavilion but the ground is dominated by the fading charms of the interesting old wooden pavilion with a central scorebox turret. The concrete practice nets are to right of the old pavilion and, beyond the woods, trains still run along the raised embankment. The ground, opened in 1878, is elliptically proportioned but the outfield is somewhat uneven.

The Olive & Partington (paperwork's company) ground is on top of a hill off Primrose Lane and is used by Glossop Juniors F.C. as a practice ground. In between the old cricket ground and the current football ground is a large 'redgra' arena with markings for several different sporting activities. Cricket has not been played here for many years but it still retains the classic oval shape of a cricket ground. As well as the Olive & Partington

works team, the ground was also used by Hadfield St Charles C.C. who were the last occupants when they folded in 1975.
The Dinting Vale ground was last used by the Calico Printers Association in the 1960's. This was a sloping ground with rough turf. There was a small pavilion at the top of the ground with distinctive white and green stripes. The ground is now the car park of Carpenters factory.
The Woods Mill works team played on a ground off Green Lane in Simmondley but is long disappeared underneath housing.
Brookfield cricket ground at Woolley Lane on the Cheshire border is now an entirely undistinguishable part of an industrial estate. The ground was last used in the 1960's.
The Maconochies works ground was on the Main Road next to the Padfield Water Treatment Works. It was a rough field when used for cricket in the 1950's and it still is.
The Field Head cricket ground in Whitfield, located somewhere behind the Beehive Public House, was used by the Littlemoor Chapel team.

GRASSMOOR

Barnes Park, N.C.B. Training Centre

Barnes Park is bordered on two sides by Birkin Lane and North Wingfield Road and the plain, stone-faced pavilion is tucked into the corner at the junction. The main entrance to the park is further down North Wingfield Road and the war memorial is the first thing you see when entering the ground (the park was built in the early 1920's as a war memorial). A tarmac path leads to the pavilion and this boundary is adorned by numerous holly and Lombardy poplar trees. On the opposite side, the boundary is marked by a wire fence and the Birkin Lane boundary is also lined with trees (though less populous than the North Wingfield Road boundary). The playing area is quite small and gently slopes away from the square towards the North East and North West boundaries. The outfield on the war memorial side is shared with the football pitch that runs parallel with North Wingfield Road.
Grassmoor was the location for the N.C.B Training Centre, a large complex of buildings with two superbly constructed sports fields. The cricket field was the lower of the two fields overlooking

the main road. The field is banked all around with steps leading down from the buildings above. Lamps run all along one boundary. The turf is now overgrown and the training centre has transmuted into the Temple Normanton Business Park. This ground could still be an outstanding venue for a top-quality cricket club.

GREAT LONGSTONE

Recreation Ground

The recreation ground in Great Longstone is in the centre of the village and is known as 'The Meadows'. The ground, that caters for football and tennis as well as cricket, is surrounded on three sides by a dry stone wall with housing all around. The old wooden pavilion, painted white, is now used as a tea-room with a more modern timber pavilion alongside. There is a freestanding scoreboard next to the old pavilion. The ground slopes into the football pitch on the far side.

GRINDLEFORD

Bridge Field, Haywood

A happy confluence of a new village playing field and the village football team forming a cricket club meant that the summer game was re-established in Grindleford around twenty years after the old club had folded. The current Grindleford C.C. share the Bridge Field with football and the Bishop Pavilion, opened in 1984, also serves as the community centre. The imposing stone built pavilion is clearly more important to the community than the ground itself and it does not face the cricket square. As a consequence, spectators on the pavilion balcony are forced to crane their necks to see the cricket. The football ground is tucked away on the far side at a strange angle to the cricket square and the pavilion. The Derwent runs behind the ground opposite the pavilion but is hidden by a row of mature trees. The river dictates the shape of the ground giving narrow straight and long square boundaries.

The old Grindleford club played on a rustic ground prone to bogginess at Haywood. This ground, dating from the latter part of the nineteenth century, was abandoned in 1958. The playing area, bounded by stone walls and fences, was long and narrow with a prodigious slope although the square in the middle of the field was completely level and is still obvious even now. There was a simple wooden pavilion. The outfield is studded with millstone grit boulders of various sizes and the larger ones, some of them very substantial, were once dynamited by the cricket club. The barely visible concrete strip once used for the practice net is the only physical remnant of cricket.

HADFIELD

St Andrews, John Walton

The only current ground in Hadfield belongs to Hadfield St Andrews C.C. The noise of the traffic on Newshaw Lane is muffled by a row of trees along the boundary and there are football pitches on two sides (although they do not form part of the outfield). There is an undistinguished modern pavilion with a motor shed and scorebox alongside in front of the car park. The nice metal gates at the entrance are probably the most stylish aspect of this rather featureless ground. The other 'church' side in Hadfield, St Charles, played their cricket on grounds in Glossop and Dinting.

Just along Newshaw Lane was the ground of the John Walton Company. This was a large ground with a pavilion at the bottom end. The club ceased to exist in 1964 and the ground has been landscaped into a two-tier recreation ground with a children's play area and a tarmac path running through the middle.

HARDWICK

Hardwick Hall

Friendly cricket is still played on the rustic, undulating ground in the grounds of the famous Elizabethan mansions. The lengthy but narrow playing area is bounded by a stone wall along the hall side and by wire fencing along the others. There are two simple wooden structures and a toilet on the hall boundary. Sheep are grazed on the pitch when not in use for cricket.

HARTSHORNE

Rodney Meadows, Spring Farm

Hartshorne Cricket Ground is an ideal place to watch cricket on a warm summer Sunday. It is behind the Admiral Rodney public house and the cricketers take their tea in the hostelry itself (sometimes on the patio between pub and cricket ground on hot days). The charm factor was diminished when the quaint but primitive pavilion on the far side of the ground was flattened but part of the boundary is still circled by a white picket fence. The ground is oval and slightly askew from the pub. The straight boundaries are average in size but the sides are very tight (only eighty-five yards across at the widest point). The ground is owned by the brewery but is leased to the cricket club for a peppercorn rent and club memorabilia can be found in a nook of the pub.

An Ordnance Survey map of the 1950's shows a cricket ground in the middle of a field to the North of the Admiral Rodney at Spring Farm. Unfortunately, we have been unable to elicit any information about this ground.

HATHERSAGE

Baulk Lane

Hathersage cricket ground is approached down the rustic, unmade, Baulk Lane. There is a tiny car park next to the stone pavilion opened in 1999. Looking out from the pavilion, that is not quite aligned properly with the massive square that accounts for two thirds the total width of the ground, there are trees to the right that hide the brook and a hedge to the left along Baulk Lane. On the opposite boundary to the pavilion is an artificial surface inside the boundary lines with new housing behind. One of the householders has constructed some steps down onto the ground from his back garden – a welcome departure from the usual hostility shown by neighbours of cricket grounds. In one corner of the ground, next to the brook, there is an air-raid type building made of brick with a barreled roof.

HATTON

Scropton Road

The village playing fields are down a short drive off Scropton Road. The cricket field was in front of the large brick changing rooms and clubhouse but has now been appropriated for a second football pitch. This was primarily due to a lack of interest in cricket by local people as the last club to play on the ground,

Hatton Q.C.C., consisted of the remnants of Qualcast C.C. who once had a ground of their own in Derby. The club folded in 1999 due to dwindling numbers after a depressing sequence of relegations. In addition to the football pitches, there is a bowling green and children's playground.

HAYFIELD

Royal Hotel

Hayfield C.C. was formed in 1859 and moved to their present ground in 1871. It is situated near the centre of the village behind the car park of the eighteenth century Royal Hotel. A very impressive pavilion complete with balcony looks over the ground with houses on both sides peeping over a whitewashed wall. The River Sett flows down the right hand side of the ground. The principal drawback to this otherwise pleasant ground is the huge hump down one side that was caused by the laying of a pipeline from a nearby reservoir. Inside the boundary on the far side of the ground is an artificial strip and three or four turf practice strips.

HEAGE

Rectory Field, Thomas Williams Playing Field

Cricket was played in Heage as long ago as 1873 on the Bullock Field close to the Tavern car park. In 1929 the club moved to a new ground in a field North of the rectory and in 1936 a five-compartment railway carriage was converted into changing rooms and pavilion. Heage left this ground in 1957. The Rectory was demolished to make way for the headquarters of the Bowmer & Kirkland Construction Company. The cricket ground is beyond this and remains a green space. The location of the square is the very obvious flat plateau in the middle of the undulating field. The pavilion is no longer there and the field is used for grazing sheep.

The cricket club re-located to Whitemoor at Belper but returned to the village in the early 1960's and played on the Thomas Williams Playing Field on Old Road. The club disbanded in 1985 and it is now only used for football. This is a small ground with sharp banking on three sides (two grassed and one with bushes). The old wooden cricket pavilion in one of the far corners has been demolished and replaced with an octagonal, brick built, metal roofed council building with no windows – functional but uninspiring.

HEANOR

Town Ground, Miners Welfare

The Town Ground on Mayfield Avenue was gifted to the people of Heanor by the wealthy Mundy family of nearby Shipley Hall and was opened in 1864. This is a long narrow ground used for football and cricket (the football pitch runs right up along the edge of the square). In addition to the expected floodlights on the football side, there are also floodlight pylons around the cricket side of the ground because 'night' matches were played in the 1980's. Derbyshire played their only first class game at Heanor in 1987 although the cricket end boundaries are barely adequate for top class amateur cricket. The turf is kept in immaculate condition particularly on the cricket side but the ground does slope slightly towards the bowling green. There are separate buildings for changing rooms, a tea room and the social club that is owned by the football club. The tall wooden scorebox painted black on the opposite side to the social club has been recently replaced by a smaller version.

The large ground of Heanor Grammar School off Ilkeston Road was never used for senior cricket but the Miners Welfare Ground, in front of the Grammar School Ground, was briefly used by Langley C.C. between 1957 and 1961. The Miners Welfare was established in 1925 and the sports field was large and flat and ran up to the main road. Cricket was rendered virtually impossible in 1968 when part of the field was taken up by the construction of the new fire station. The other strip of land running parallel to Ilkeston Road was later used to build flats. The greatly reduced remaining turf is now used for junior football and is only accessible through the car park of the Miner's Welfare.

HEATH

Heath Comprehensive School

The sports field of Heath Comprehensive School was used by Holmewood M.W.C.C. whilst they were waiting for their new ground to be built in the early 1980's. The entire school, opened as recently as 1963, was totally demolished in the 1990's and housing has been built over most of the area it occupied.

HILTON

Marston Lane End

This is an old ground (1879) with considerable potential. The area of the ground is big enough to accommodate two pitches and is completely flat. There is a large flat roofed pavilion (slightly askew to the boundaries of the ground), motor sheds and a practice net (rubber on concrete). The playing surface is marked out in an oval and is 150 yards from side to side. The straight boundaries from the pavilion to the main road are a little shorter. However the entrance to the ground off Marston Lane End is the site of an ugly looking, albeit small, electricity sub-station and the ground is completely open with very few trees or even shrubbery on the boundary edges. The advent of the A50 has managed to reduce the constant hum of traffic on Derby Road to bearable levels.

HOLBROOK

Holbrook Hall

The drive leading to Holbrook Hall, now an old people's home, off Makeney Road had a football ground on the left and a cricket ground on the right. The football ground survives as the home of Holbrook St Michaels F.C. but the cricket ground, once the home of Holbrook Park C.C. is now a grazing field for cattle. The grounds were known as 'The Parks' and were last used for cricket in 1962.

HOLMESFIELD

Robin Hood Inn, Cordwell Lane

Holmesfield C.C. have played at two different grounds in two different hamlets. Their original ground was next to the Robin Hood Inn at Lydgate. Both the inn and ground are now in private hands and not used for their original purpose. It was a very small and uneven playing surface and boundaries to one section of wall only counted two runs. The club abandoned this ground in 1959 and moved to a new location at Millthorpe.

The layout of the new ground is almost identical to that of Hathersage. The outfield is rough and slopes towards trees at the bottom that obscure a brook. The total area of the two grounds is almost equivalent but Holmesfield has more uneven dimensions (the straight boundaries are longer than the square boundaries). Both grounds have marvellous new pavilions. The Holmesfield pavilion has just been built from bricks with stone facing and a slate roof. The tiny old wooden structure in the bottom corner of the ground is still standing but now looks a little shabby. Unlike Hathersage, this ground is completely surrounded by open countryside (apart from Carr Lane along one boundary). Trees form a natural border on two sides but a neat wooden fence marks the other two boundaries.

HOLMEWOOD

Colliery Ground, Community Centre Playing Fields

Hardwick Colliery, formed in 1936, had a good-sized ground at Williamthorpe almost in the shadow of the pit heads. The pavilion was large wooden building with a verandah and a balcony raised above ground level. They later became Hardwick & Holmewood M.W.C.C. but their splendid ground was purchased by Derbyshire County Council in 1979 for use as an industrial estate. The entire colliery area, including the ground, is now submerged beneath the industrial estate and the industrial units that stand directly above the former cricket field are, almost mockingly, called Pavilion Workshops. As a sop to the cricket club the Council agreed to establish a new cricket pitch in the centre of the village but the club moved to the sports field of Heath Comprehensive School until the new facility was available in 1982.

The new ground is situated off Old Colliery Lane close to the centre of the village behind the Miners Welfare building. This is a long but rather narrow ground sharing with football. The changing rooms are hidden away behind a hedge and the bowling green close to the community centre building. There is an older building on the ground built of brick blocks painted black that doubles as a motor shed and scorebox. Close to this building is a strip of concrete that was once an artificial practice wicket. There are trees and bushes on both the straight boundaries but for the most part they are scrubby and unprepossessing.

HOLYMOORSIDE

Recreation Ground

Holymoorside, who had a cricket team in the 1950's, played on a pleasant if primitive little ground below the Bulls Head public house next to the bridge over the River Hipper. Football is still played on the pitch but it is a small area with no room for expansion (river, road, trees and banking form natural boundaries). The ground dates from about 1920. Hipper Hall Farm had been sold to Charles Markham and he gave Mill Holme Field to the parish. Another local worthy, Sir Ernest Shentall, paid for the field to be levelled. In 1924, Sir Ernest presented a wooden sectional building that had been his nut store (he owned a wholesale fruit and vegetable business) to be used as the village hall on the hill at the top of the ground. The changing rooms next to the hall were added shortly after by the Miners Welfare Commission.

HOPE

Cement Works, Hope Valley College

The Blue Circle cement works (formerly known as G & T Earle) was built in 1929 and is home to a superb sports and leisure facility. In addition to the regulation football, tennis and bowls they also have a golf course. Tideswell C.C. used the ground in recent years but it is now only occasionally used for casual staff games. As part of the golf course, the turf is in magnificent condition and the wonderful Art-deco style pavilion is a protected building and now used as the football changing rooms. It was designed for the 1929 R.H.S. show at Manchester to showcase 'Snowcrete', a product of the new works. The plans are dated May 1932 and the building was presumably constructed around this time. It also provides a rather large hazard to the golfers - almost 'crazy golf' on a vast scale.

Cricket was played in the 1970's on the sports field of Hope Valley College (founded 1958) on Castleton Road by a team of students called the Hope Valley Cavaliers. This is currently used for rugby and football but the concrete strips once used for cricket nets are still there. The cement works are visible through the hills facing away from the college buildings.

HOPTON

Hopton Hall

Looking at the former home of Hopton & Carsington C.C. today, it is almost unimaginable how cricket could have been played here. It is a ravine with tree-lined hills on three sides and the high brick wall of the Hopton Hall grounds on the roadside. The players changed in the dairy farm next to the ground. There is an old icehouse used by the hall in the field. It is unlikely that cricket has been played here since 1955.

HUNDALL

Sunnyside Meadow

Sunnyside Meadow, home to Hundall C.C. since at least 1912, is on the junction of Windmill Lane and Hundall Lane although the corner of the junction is occupied by a pub, some houses and a small sewage works. The stone car park at the entrance is well constructed and the newer and larger of two wooden pavilions is tucked into this corner of the ground. The smaller structure is partly concealed by trees to the left. There is a concrete practice area behind the pavilion. The ground has a big slope on the pavilion side but levels out past the square towards the hedged boundary of Hundall Lane. The far boundary has a wooden fence beyond some scrubland (the boundary is mown into an oval shape on what is basically a square ground). The square is offset towards Hundall Lane to avoid the slopes on the pavilion side but this unfortunately unbalances the ground. The cricket club obtained a long-term lease on the ground when the Whitbread Brewery sold the nearby Miners Arms public house.

IDRIDGEHAY

Wirksworth Road

The small sports field on Wirksworth Road was once used for hockey and cricket but is now a football pitch. The concrete foundation blocks for the old wooden pavilion remain near the entrance. The ground is currently enclosed by a wire fence and the entrance is open although the old gateposts are still standing. There are plenty of trees around the edges of the ground with a small copse at the northern end. The views are pretty on all sides.

ILKESTON

Rutland Recreation Ground, Ilkeston School (two separate grounds), Bennerley Recreation Ground, St John Houghton School, Kirk Hallam Community School, South East Derbyshire College, Gallows Inn Playing Fields, The Stute, Notts & Derby Power, The Ropewalk, Cotmanhay Playing Fields, A.Booth & Son, Manners Colliery

The principal venue for cricket in Ilkeston is 'The Rec'; a huge ground gifted to the people of Ilkeston by the Duke of Rutland. This provenance is reflected in the official name of the ground, The Rutland Recreation Ground, and the name of the most important club that play on it, Ilkeston Rutland C.C., one of the oldest clubs in Derbyshire founded in 1829. The club had played on two other grounds in the town and moved to the current ground in the 1880's. Their previous ground near St Mary's Church was described as one of the prettiest in England and a painting of the match between the All England XI and XXII of Ilkeston and District in 1851 is owned by the M.C.C. The current ground is so big (some twenty acres) that even Derbyshire did not play to the full boundaries and the playing surface is perfectly level, though perhaps the quality of the turf has suffered since it was abandoned by county cricket. The Duke of Rutland offered the ground to Ilkeston Borough Council in 1914 as a memorial to the visit of King George V on condition that it would be improved and made suitable for county cricket. The Duke also limited the amount of buildings that could be built on the land with important unforeseen consequences. The plans to develop the ground were delayed by the war until the 1920's. A new pavilion was constructed and Derbyshire first played here in 1925. Nottinghamshire were the first opponents and it became the traditional venue for this fixture, attracting five figure crowds after the war. Recently, Erewash Borough Council, despite heated local protests, decided to build a sports centre on the western boundary and a tennis centre halfway along the eastern boundary. Because of the good intentions of the Duke of Rutland other buildings had to be sacrificed. The excellent terracing in front of the pavilion has been torn away and replaced with a set of metal steps and the superb, whitewashed, brick scorebox on the southern boundary has been demolished. The pavilion is still an imposing structure but it seems to be disfigured without the terracing. The lower half of the building is used for ground machinery. The entrance turnstile, half concealed by shrubbery, in the North West corner of the ground remains but is unlikely to be used again.

Behind the pavilion, across West End Drive, is Ilkeston School (formerly the Grammar School) opened in 1914. Their small pitch was directly opposite the Recreation ground and was used by Old Ilkestonians C.C. on a regular basis until the 1970's and by the now defunct Ilkeston Park Avenue club from 1977 until the ground was built over by classroom blocks in 1984. However their new pitch, West of the school, has been used in recent years for 3rd XI cricket. The outfield doubles as two football pitches in winter. A running track forms a useful boundary but restricts the playing area. The lone artificial pitch favoured by state schools in recent years happily gave way to a small turf square in 2000 and the ground has now been fenced off to protect against vandals and the bowel movements of local dogs. The sports master is pursuing the possibility of a pavilion in situ to avoid the long trudge down from the school changing rooms.

Bennerley School playing fields, now fortified by vicious metal fencing on three sides with the school buildings acting as a guard to the fourth side, were once shared by the school pupils and the general public of Cotmanhay for football and cricket. Derbyshire County Council, invoking the 1944 Education Act, took them from the control of Erewash Borough Council and installed incompetent Groundstaff. This quickly resulted in a deterioration of the cricket square that forced Cotmanhay Church C.C. (who had used the ground since the late nineteenth century) to disband in 1951. A team called Cotmanhay briefly used the ground in the late 1980's but otherwise the school pupils have been the only cricketers to use the wide-open spaces that are little changed since it was a public park. The ground can be seen from across the Erewash Canal, which runs along the eastern boundary.

St John Houghton School was opened in 1965, but their playing fields did not open until the following year. The sports ground, behind the gymnasium, is long and narrow with room for three football pitches side-by-side. There is an artificial strip in between the first two football grounds nearest the gym that allows for run-ups but the surrounding turf is very rough. The views are far from inspiring with a metal fence to the left, housing to the right and a power station straight ahead. On the credit side, they have a wooden scorebox in front of the ground and concrete practice strips around the corner of the school buildings. This venue has been used in recent years for 3rd XI cricket.

Kirk Hallam Community School and Kirk Hallam Community Technology College share the same site with two different entrances. The sports fields are on the Ilkeston side of the site and are virtually next to the main Derby Road. The cricket pitch, situated next to the rugby pitch, was used by Cotmanhay C.C. in the 1980's (the team was eventually re-christened Kirk Hallam & Cotmanhay C.C. in 1991). More recently it was used by West Hallam White Rose C.C. as a venue for their 3rd XI. The ground is surrounded by mature trees and is large but parts of the outfield are shared with rugby and cricket. There is a solitary artificial wicket in a poor state of repair and no square (senior cricket has not been played on turf here). The whole playing fields are strewn with litter and local people are evidently fond of using the facility as a dog toilet. Six old concrete practice strips, pitted with grass, remain behind the goalposts on the football pitch nearest the college buildings.

Ilkeston College of Further Education was opened in 1954 replacing the old town institute. This later became the South East Derbyshire College. The college playing field, used by Cotmanhay C.C. in the mid-1980's, would make an effective cricket ground but for the presence of football. The playing area is spacious, enclosed on all sides by walls, fencing or steep banks. Concrete steps lead onto the ground from the college buildings above.

Very much a secondary facility to the Recreation Ground, but still owned and maintained by Erewash Borough Council, are the Gallows Inn Playing Fields sandwiched between the Erewash

Canal and the River Erewash (the boundary with Nottinghamshire). Gallows Inn 1 is easily the better of these two pitches. It is a perfect oval with long boundaries and completely encircled with a concrete path. The basic structure and design of the pavilion is also pleasing but it is cursed by the need to protect from vandalism (metal shutters for example). On the far side of the playing fields, Gallows Inn 2 is very much the poor relation. The outfield is shared with a football pitch and the pavilion is dingy and ugly.

Ilkeston Rugby Club were based on the pitch between Nottingham Road and Gallows Inn 1 and this is still used for rugby but the club have now made the Stanton Institute (commonly known as 'The Stute') their new headquarters. As a consequence the cricket square is sandwiched between two rugby pitches (one senior and one junior). The Stanton Ironworks company opened the institute in 1937 and their cricket team was, for a number of years after the war, the strongest in Ilkeston. Local people first used the playing fields in the 1880's but they were purchased and improved by the Stanton Company and officially opened in 1931. The substantial and attractive wooden pavilion with a scorebox in the roof is still used as changing rooms but it all looks rather forlorn these days.

A number of Ilkeston cricket grounds have disappeared since the war. The Notts & Derby Power Company Ground was on Station Road and is now Smiths Garage. A short walk from this ground, at the end of Ropewalk, was the ground of Nutbrook. This is now a field containing a few bedraggled horses and, at the time of writing, was for sale. Ironically, the Notts & Derby Power Company team moved to West Hallam in 1948, became the East Midland Electricity Board, and eventually sold their ground to the nomadic Nutbrook club (see the section on West Hallam for details of this ground).

Nutbrook also briefly played on Cotmanhay Playing Fields, a sports ground constructed on the land of the old Hopewell Farm. This large ground now accommodates three football pitches and a basketball court and is flanked by a railway line on the far side and the sprawling housing estate on all other sides. Two gaudy murals almost certainly designed by children (we hope) decorate the plain brick changing rooms.

The sports ground built by the textile manufacturer A.Booth & Son is on Awsworth Road diagonally opposite the New Manor Ground (home of Ilkeston Town F.C.). This was a fine ground with enough room for cricket and football to be played side-by-side although the straight boundaries are short of the ideal. Locked between the Erewash Canal and the railway line, in the shadow of Bennerley Viaduct; a magnificent wrought iron Victorian construction that reaches up to 60ft, this unusual location is now only used for football. The ground opened in July 1951 but the company only fielded a cricket team until the end of the 1956 season.
At the turn of the nineteenth century, Manners Colliery C.C. were the kings of Derbyshire cricket and their ground, opened in 1892, was located next to the colliery itself. The Colliery was later renamed Ilkeston Colliery and was the last pit in Ilkeston when it closed in 1949. This whole area bears no traces of its mining heritage and the colliery land is now the Manners Industrial Estate. The ground was last used in the 1950's by Old Park C.C. and is now known as Manners Playing Fields. There are two football pitches and modern changing rooms built in the usual practical but perfunctory style of council buildings.

KEDLESTON

Playing Fields

Kedleston Playing Fields was on the junction of Mercaston Lane and Lodge Lane in the village close to the rectory and was originally known as Thistley Field. A wooden pavilion was sited approximately halfway down the Mercaston Lane boundary. The old cricket ground is now indivisible from an adjoining field (once a separate piece of land called Thistley Close) and a telephone line now runs diagonally across the cricket end of the field.

KILLAMARSH

Sheffield Road

The Killamarsh Young Boys Association was formed just before the First World War and by the 1920's they had their own sports field on former marshland off Sheffield Road. In 1926 they added a wooden pavilion and coke waste was used to raise the football field on a slightly higher plateau than the cricket field. Many years later, this ground is now a quite splendid sports facility still entirely owned by the Killamarsh Juniors Sports Club. The old pavilion has been improved and extended with new changing rooms. Between the buildings and the cricket field is an excellent tarmac car park and a line of seats for spectators. The outfield is lovingly maintained with a high standard of turf although there is a ridge before the edge of the square that has an artificial strip at the pavilion edge. The right hand boundary is a high hedge and the left hand boundary is a grass embankment with the railway line behind that runs along the dividing line that separates Derbyshire from Yorkshire. The football pitch beyond the cricket pitch is fenced off and entirely distinct. Although the club is known as Killamarsh Juniors they are a senior sports organisation with a licensed bar within the pavilion.

KIRK LANGLEY

Barrington Cricket Field

The Barrington Cricket Field is found down The Cunnery; a road name that is almost impossible to say with a straight face. This is a typical village ground that borders on lovingly tended back gardens, open fields and the church (St Michael's). The ground is divided from the churchyard by a ha-ha. The inexplicably cramped modern pavilion is on the opposite side of the ground. This is now being extended but is by no means aesthetically sympathetic to the rustic ground. The outfield is heavily undulated but the demise of football may improve the condition of the turf. The wickets have been recently pitched North South as opposed to the traditional East West axis. This has ensured that the much longer boundaries are now straight rather than square. As its name may suggest, the ground was donated to the village by the Barrington family.

LANGLEY MILL

Station Road, The Meadow

Langley Mill United C.C. was formed in 1870 and has a most distinguished record on the field of play. They were instrumental in the formation of the Border League and, until recently, were members of the Derbyshire Premier League. Their ground is on the busy main road through Langley Mill but leylandii trees

planted along the boundary behind the venerable wooden fence completely masks the ground from public view for this was a club that charged an entrance fee to watch the cricket. The outfield slopes from the main road down to the pavilion. In many locations this building would be an abomination but in this urban setting next to an industrial estate, it seems appropriately harsh and functional. It is large, built of red brick with a balcony on the upper floor looking out onto the field of play. LMUCC is picked out in darker bricks on the side face nearest the main entrance on Amber Drive. The turf is in excellent condition and all the facilities are more than adequate but this is a ground that will never transcend its cheerless surroundings.
Langley Mill School was established in 1909 and their sports field, behind the school building, was known as The Meadow. The ground, directly to the South of Bailey Brook, was used by Mansfield Road Methodists and Langley C.C. The school was closed and Langley left in 1956 to play on the Miners Welfare Ground in Heanor. The school is now Chris Roads Garage and the sports field is a boggy, overgrown wilderness barely accessible from Aldred's Lane. A solitary football post is all that is left to indicate that this was anything other than waste ground.

LANGWITH

Main Street

Langwith cricket ground was opened in 1907 to coincide with the club moving from the Scarcliffe and District League into the Bassetlaw League. It was built on top of cottage gardens with a circular cinder track and a railed fence around the boundary. The club and ground declined through the 1970's and 1980's as a consequence of the pit closures and the accompanying social deprivation. The original pavilion was destroyed by arsonists in 1980 and the ground was plagued by vandalism. It is difficult to judge Langwith cricket ground objectively because this is a poverty-stricken area - the brutal looking brick changing rooms are surrounded by a steel cage. The once impressive tall brick scorebox has recently been demolished. The playing surface is long and narrow with dips and undulations and the turf is far from pristine. There is a Methodist church on the opposite side of the ground to the changing rooms so perhaps they may pray for the restoration of the club and ground and the fortunes of the people that live around it.

LEA

Lea Mills

Lea Mills were built by Peter Nightingale, a rival of Arkwright, at the birth of the industrial revolution and still survive as a going concern. The works sports ground is close to the building but is currently unused. It is a sharply sloping and undulating field with an earthwork halfway up in an attempt to level the football field. There are dry stone walls on the two long side boundaries and looking out from the distressed wooden pavilion at the top of the ground, there are wonderful views of tree-lined hills. The slopes and bumps are so severe that it is hard to imagine either serious football or cricket games taking place here nowadays.

LEABROOKS

Crays Hill

One would normally congratulate local councils for forming cricket grounds but Crays Hill Recreation Ground is a disaster. The ground was once Leabrooks Tip and was leveled and turfed over to form a cricket and football ground. Somercotes Casuals were the first team to play here in 1981. They eventually disbanded and it became a venue for 3rd XI cricket. Unfortunately the ground began to subside, was abandoned after the 1998 season and it is now a hilly wilderness mainly used by dog walkers. The brutal, windowless, brick pavilion serves as a reminder of the cricket ground that is no more. However, Amber Valley Borough Council are planning to reopen this ground in 2005 (although the square will be in a different part of the field).

LINTON

Rickman's Corner

The ground is located at Rickmans Corner and was originally established in the nineteenth century as the colliery cricket ground. The ground is square and smallish with one corner sliced off to house two wooden pavilions, one of which is used by the Linton Community Sports and Activity Centre (formed in

1994 according to the sign) as a play group for small children. Even the football pitch does not appear to be used anymore and the last cricket club to use the ground was the once powerful Old Netherseal Colliery C.C.

LITTLE EATON

St Peter's Park

St Peter's Park is a busy place with facilities for cricket, football, bowls and tennis. The presence of a football pitch means that the cricket square is uncomfortably close to the narrowing width of the ground near the pavilion. The other side of the square is also used for junior football so the outfield is rutted on both sides. The building that houses the tearoom and changing rooms doubles as a doctor's surgery during the week. The ground is bordered on two sides by Church Road and Duffield Road and there are dry stone walls along the entire length of these boundaries. There is a concrete practice surface opposite the pavilion on the Duffield Road boundary. The monument next to the pavilion looks like a war memorial from afar but it actually commemorates the coronation of George V in 1913. The cricket club was formed in 1862 but the ground was gifted to the people of the parish by Mr Thomas Bates in 1902.

LONG EATON & SAWLEY

West Park, Trent College, Vida, Long Eaton School (two separate grounds), Charles Street, Copsey Croft, Sawley (Trent Bridge, Sawley Park, Concordia)

Long Eaton is a lucky town. In the midst of their shops, streets and houses they have a magnificent sporting facility called West Park. Cricketers are particularly lucky because the wide expanses of the park house a number of cricket pitches and at least two of them are outstanding. The first section of the park was purchased by the Long Eaton Urban District Council in December 1905 and it was sometimes referred to as the Kings Ground. At this time the two foremost venues for cricket in the town were the Queens Ground just to the North of Trent College and the Recreation Ground off Nottingham Road, both of which had been opened in the 1880's. Established around the same time as West Park was Red Roe Field at Longmoor Farm. West

Park was sometimes criticized for the usual faults of public parks like poor pitches and no proper boundaries and, before the war, it was shunned by many senior clubs in the area. However, it grew in size, outlived the other grounds and survived, in better shape than ever, to this day.

Long Eaton C.C were formed as recently as 1973 when Long Eaton Old Boys merged with Vida, and their pitch near the cemetery is also a merger, between what the council called Pitch 1 and Pitch 2. A tree lined asphalt path circles most of the pitch that was first used in its present form in 1972. The playing surface is huge, especially from the tennis courts to the factory end. The harsh looking brick pavilion, fortified as a protection against vandalism, is in the corner next to the bowling green. The LECC monogram in contrasting brick was covered with black sprayed graffiti when we visited the ground. A pleasing feature, incidental to the playing of cricket, is the bandstand in the opposite corner to the pavilion.

Next to Long Eaton's pitch is another huge expanse of turf. It is bordered on two sides by the Erewash Canal and Long Eaton Cemetery forms another fairly immovable boundary. Once again, this area is large enough to accommodate two cricket pitches but there is one square in the middle. The changing rooms for this pitch, sited in the corner of the ground where the Cemetery meets the canal, were pulled down in the last few years and replaced with a skateboard rink. This pitch was most recently used by Sawley 3rd XI and for youth cricket. The cricket pitch towards the centre of the park, nearest Trent College, is circular, surrounded by a path with no changing rooms. There is an attractive whitewashed shelter with vaguely art deco styling next to the ground.

The two pitches on the Sawley side of West Park are really three in disguise since there is a square, used for junior matches, between the boundaries of the pitch nearest the swimming baths (the home of Sawley & Long Eaton Park C.C.), and the pitch that was the former home of Long Eaton Park (before their merger with Sawley). Both pitches have pavilions although the rather basic brick structure on the old Long Eaton Park pitch is likely to decline now it does not have an autonomous club to care for it. The Sawley pavilion has grown in size and improved as a facility since the formation of the Derbyshire Premier League in 1999. Perhaps Erewash Borough Council could be persuaded to re-site the rugby pitches that affect the outfield of this important pitch to another part of West Park. The Sawley club are keen to maintain their status as a premier club and this venue should be able to rival that of Long Eaton C.C. at the other end of the park. There are plenty of mature trees around the periphery but perhaps some form of permanent boundary around the playing area (a fence, bushes, advertising hoardings) would militate against the 'public park' atmosphere. Both the pitches at the Sawley end are substantial in size but rather smaller than their counterparts across the park.

Trent College is situated to the North of West Park and was founded in 1868. Cricket commenced the following season. The college has four cricket squares but three of them are part of the same lengthy piece of turf that runs parallel to Golden Brook. The main square is between two rugby pitches close to the Standbury Pavilion, a modern but relatively stylish building opened by the sportswriter Alan Lee in 1990. This replaced an antiquated wooden building situated near the current practice nets. To the West of the main pitch is Turner Fields, a reasonably sized pitch with small wooden changing rooms and to the East is The Spinney, a very restricted area only used by the youngest elevens of the school. The other pitch is between rugby pitches on the top level of the school grounds next to the school buildings (known as 'Top Fields'). Derbyshire played five John Player league matches on the main pitch between 1975 and 1979. The main protagonists in bringing county cricket to the ground were the headmaster, A.J.Maltby, who was eager to publicise his school; and Fred Perks, a local businessman. The first match attracted a large crowd estimated at around 6,000, a Derbyshire record at the time.

The Jones Stroud Company established a ground for their factory team Vida in 1958 on part of the 48 acre Oakleys farm site. According to Keith Breakwell in his comprehensive history of Long Eaton cricket "The Acton Close ground was lovely...it was large, flat, out in the country, had a characterful pavilion, a true playing surface." Excellent practice facilities were added in 1964 but the land was too valuable to remain a cricket ground and after the 1971 season it was sold. It is now underneath an industrial estate. When Vida merged with the Old Boys, their wooden pavilion was re-erected on West Park. This pavilion was eventually replaced by the current brick structure discussed above.

Long Eaton School was opened in October 1910 as the Long Eaton County School and cricket was probably played by the school side the following year. An Old Boys XI played on the small school ground in the early 1920's and then in the 1930's as Old Lecssians C.C. The school was renamed Long Eaton Grammar School after the Second World War and the old boys team became L.E.G.S.O.B.C.C. After the 1957 season, the ground was taken for new school buildings and the current sports field was not available until the early 1960's. This is a typical unenclosed and featureless school playing field catering for multiple sports and is sandwiched between the school buildings and the canal. Neither ground has ever had any substantial buildings for the purpose of changing and watching the game under cover. As noted above, the Old Boys club eventually became Long Eaton C.C. with their own pitch on West Park. The only senior club to use the school grounds in recent years were Olympians C.C. in the late 1970's.

The cricket ground at Charles Street has been partly built over and the rump of the ground, now cut off from Charles Street by Manchester Street, is used for football. It was opened in the 1930's and until the Second World War was the home of the Cobden C.C. After the war, the Discharged Soldiers and Sailors club used the ground with some of the Cobden players in their team. Over five hundred spectators crowded onto the ground in 1956 when the home team took on a Derbyshire XI for George Dawkes' testimonial fund.

Long Eaton Co-op had a ground at the end of Recreation Street felicitously named Copsey Croft. This was a good ground with an excellent square. It was later taken over by Nottingham Victoria Control C.C. who changed their name to Copsey Croft C.C. prior to abandoning the ground in the late 1970's (they moved onto West Park). The playing surface had declined with the death of the groundsman and has been recently built over by new housing. One of the courts is named Copsey Croft.

The old Sawley Cricket Club (sometimes it was known as Old Sawley C.C.) played on a crude ground behind the Harrington Arms. This ground was basically a cow field alongside the banks of the River Trent and, amusingly when compared to its illustrious namesake, it was called Trent Bridge Cricket Ground. The pavilion, at the pub end, was an old shed. The ground was used by the club from at least 1868 until their demise in 1960. The field is still there.
Of more recent vintage is Sawley Park off Draycott Road (opened in 1964). This large field, adjacent to a Sawley Infants & Junior School, now comprises two football pitches. There are modern changing rooms and the playing area is still in good condition but the square has disappeared. Sawley Parkside C.C. left this ground in 1977 and West Park is likely to remain the venue of choice for cricketers in Sawley. The Concordia Company had a ground off Ruskin Avenue, New Sawley, in the 1960's. This was an unremarkable ground wedged between housing and, all along the southern boundary, the railway line. It is now underneath housing (Elgar Drive runs through where the middle of the pitch would have been).

LONGCLIFFE

Viaduct

The post war home of Brassington C.C. between 1954 and 1961 was just under the railway viaduct on the right-hand side of the road before reaching the limestone works. The changing rooms were an old railway wagon on top of a bank to the left of where the playing surface used to be. This is now an unremarkable field with no trace of sporting activity. The turn into this viaduct was the one of the sharpest curves in the entire British railway network. It now forms part of the High Peak Trail & Midshires Way. Before the war, Brassington had a ground within the boundaries of the village. This was in a triangular field close to the Hoben Industrial Minerals Plant in the shadow of the Harboro Rocks (the ground was known as Harboro).

LONGFORD

Longford Hall

Cricket was played near Longford Hall until the early 1960's and was one of those grounds that Roy Christian claimed, writing in the Derbyshire Life & Countryside, "on which it was a pleasure to make a duck." The hall and estate were subsidiary possessions of the Coke family from Holkham Hall in Norfolk. The Cokes and their successors all encouraged the playing of cricket and there was an annual cricket week for many years. Mr H.A.Manners, then the owner of the estate, erected a new pavilion in 1939 and this was eventually relocated at Sutton-on-the-Hill when the Longford Hall club disbanded. The ground was probably built in the Victorian era and was to the South West of the house, enclosed by a fence within a larger field.

LOSCOE

Charles Hill, Miners Welfare

Charles Hill is a council owned facility that encompasses football pitches, a sports hall and a large cricket ground. Unusually for modern council facilities, the changing rooms overlook the cricket although the windows and main door of the original design have been bricked in. The playing area is extensive and on a plateau with splendid views of the local area. The football pitches are behind and below the cricket pitch. There is a slight slope across the field but there are no undulations. The ground is fully booked as a 3rd XI ground for local clubs.

Loscoe Colliery C.C. was among the best teams in Derbyshire in the 1920's. Their ground is situated behind the miner's welfare building but is no longer used for cricket. A football pitch, that occupies only half the spacious rectangular playing surface, is still in use but the original wooden pavilion has been replaced by two portakabins.

LULLINGTON

Edingale Lane

Lullington Park C.C. set the standards in Derbyshire club cricket with respect to planning for the future. They have built a second pitch (with an artificial wicket on the square), replaced their ageing nets with two excellent new artificial strips in between the two playing surfaces and they have good wicket covers. They run four senior teams and youth teams at every age group. The ground, continuously used by the club since at least 1881, is close to the centre of the village fenced within a field that is grazed by sheep and cattle off Edingale Lane. The animals sometimes mingle alarmingly close to parked cars in this outer field. The ground is on a plateau and affords lovely views of the rolling countryside. The church is just visible through mature trees along Edingale Lane. The club has recently constructed a grand new pavilion with a separate facade for each pitch.

MAPPERLEY

Simon Lane

Mapperley once had a cricket ground near the lodge house built by the Mundy family around the turn of the century. That ground has long disappeared but cricket was played after the Second World War on the Simon Lane Recreation Ground. The ground has hedges and open countryside on three sides with a fence on the boundary that shields a small group of unusual wooden houses. The ground is long and narrow and was last used for football. The changing rooms are in a distressed state (half the roof is missing) and the toilet in the wood at the bottom of the ground is in ruins.

MAREHAY

The Maryfield, Holly Bush Inn

Marehay have a new ground (first used in 1997) called The Maryfield almost opposite their old ground on Warmwells Lane. The field they obtained for the ground is not an ideal shape for a cricket ground and the pavilion and playing area are skewed at an angle to the main road and the large limestone chipping car park. The pavilion is large and constructed of brick with a clock and weather vane on the roof providing interest to an otherwise featureless building. The shape and size of the field constrict the playing area but even the small boundaries are adequate and it is level and flat. As yet, this ground is rather bland but there is scope for development next to the car park and in the far left-hand corner (tennis courts or bowling greens perhaps).

The old ground, opened in 1906, was certainly characterful but sadly it was far too small for modern cricket, particularly the good standard attained by the club. The ground was owned by the Holly Bush public house that backed onto the playing area. At the time of its closure there were two pavilion buildings neither of which were particularly attractive. The outfield was bumpy but well kept. The whole ground has now been built over and the housing is called 'Poppyfields'. The bowling green adjacent to the cricket field still seems to be in good order. The Maryfield is to the Holly Bush what Pride Park is to the Baseball Ground. The ground is better, the facilities are much better; but, by God, don't you miss the old atmosphere sometimes.

MARKHAM

Colliery Ground

The oval sports ground constructed by Markham Colliery had facilities for football, cricket, bowls and tennis. It fell prey to the construction of the M1 motorway and the ground is now under the motorway and the concrete yard of the Castle Hill Chemical Company.

MATLOCK

Causeway Lane, Matlock College

The sports ground in Matlock on Causeway Lane is shared by Matlock Town F.C. and Matlock C.C. The football club are interlopers because the cricket club played on the football pitch until 1911 when the footballers moved across the road from the flood prone Hall Leys Park. The cricket club shuffled along and converted the meadow next door into a new ground. The cricket area is a good size and the football pitch does not encroach onto the cricket outfield too much and is in better condition than most grounds of this nature. The old wooden pavilion perched on a high bank level with the square is entirely attractive and shows sign of recent renovation. It was constructed in the early 1890's at a cost of £120. This building is used as a bar and tearoom with the scorebox in the roof. The players change in a more recent and less pleasing building on the boundary nearest the small car park. The main road is successfully hidden by a large hawthorn hedge and the modern housing jutting out behind the

other boundaries is stone built and relatively easy on the eye. There is an artificial strip on the square and two artificial practice nets near the car park.
Matlock C.C. briefly evacuated their traditional home when the square was completely relaid in the 1970's. Their temporary base was at Matlock College to the North of Matlock Bridge near the partially derelict Rockside Hall. The former college playing fields are now owned by the Cavendish Fields Sports Association. The best of six football pitches is used by Matlock United F.C. but cricket is no longer played here. The turf is in good condition but the high altitude makes for windy weather and the superb views are almost completely obscured by the large but prosaic wooden pavilion.

MELBOURNE

Cockshut Lane

Melbourne cricket ground is part of large sports complex outside the town on Cockshut Lane. On leaving the main road there is a football pitch to the left that forms part of the cricket ground outfield and another football pitch and a rugby pitch to the right. The pitches on the right are separated from the cricket ground by a hedge. The pavilion is a large white building in front of the cricket pitch and the plaque says that the ground was given to Melbourne by the Admiral of the Fleet Lord Walter T Kerr to commemorate the First World War. There is a separate scorebox and one artificial practice net adjacent to the pavilion. The cricket club has suffered many complaints from residents in houses backing onto the ground. These are strange people who move in next to an old established cricket ground and then complain about the occasional cricket ball landing in their garden or striking their roof.

MIDDLETON

Recreation Ground

In a county cursed by bad access to cricket grounds, Middleton almost rivals the virtually impenetrable Whaley Bridge ground. Leaving Porter Lane, you drive over a rickety little bridge and down a potholed, lurching track that leads to a circular car park surrounded by rough grass. Next to the car park, along one boundary, is a bank formed by ancient mine workings. A dry stone wall in need of renovation forms the other boundaries. The first part of the field forms the cricket ground but beyond the square is a football pitch running longways (the straight boundaries are considerably longer than the very short square boundaries). The wooden pavilion is small and looks rather rickety. It was funded by public subscription after the ground was provided for the people of Middleton at a nominal rent by Mr F.C.Arkwright J.P. His wife laid the foundation stone on Whit Monday, 1889 in the presence of over 500 spectators and the Wirksworth Volunteer Brass Band. The scorebox, also wooden, aged and rickety, has a freestanding scoreboard alongside. This is a wild and unkempt ground with a bit of windswept charm. Although it is now politely known as the Recreation Ground it was once named Bedlam Field.

MILFORD

Moscow Farm

It is over fifty years since Milford Institute played cricket and their ground is now a large agricultural field next to the recreation ground on Moscow Straight. The field was owned by Moscow Farm and was an unsophisticated yet attractive venue. The ground is below the level of the main road and bordered on the opposite side by the River Derwent with pleasant views all around. The changing room was a railway carriage that backed onto the brick wall of the farm. The entrance gate and steps are still there but are acutely overgrown.

MONYASH

Horse Lane

How is it possible to pinpoint with accuracy the location of Monyash cricket ground since cricket has not been played here since the 1940's? Football was played on the same ground more recently (the 1960's perhaps) and the local residents have good memories but an old rusting roller in the corner of the field nearest the public footpath stile is the best clue of all. To find the ground, one must veer off Horse Lane and tramp up and over hilly fields and at least three stiles. Crops are now grown in the large rolling field.

MOORFIELD

Moorfield Hall

Moorfield Hall was the seat of the Hill-Wood family, players and patrons of Derbyshire county cricket and directors of Arsenal F.C. Their own private ground was in a field close to the entrance of the house. Whitfield St James used the ground before the Second World War but, according to folk memory, it was still in use in the 1950's and 1960's. It is now an overgrown field.

MORLEY

Broomfield Hall, Morley Hall

The village of Morley, to the best of our knowledge, has never had a cricket team but there was a ground at Broomfield Hall, an agricultural college. The Derbyshire Farm Institute formed a team in the 1950's and maintained a regular fixture list until 1964. The ground was off the public footpath that leads up to the Hall from the main road. The ground is quite small with a marked slope from top to bottom. The square was on an artificially raised plateau and the pavilion and concrete practice nets were located in the South West corner of the ground. Most of the field is intact and the turf is still clearly superior to that of the surrounding fields but part of the outfield at the top of the ground has been planted with trees.

A real curiosity is the seventeen-acre paddock of Morley Hall that Mike Horton, formerly chairman of the county club, has partially converted into a cricket ground. Only two or three games a year are played here which accounts for the tiny square that accommodates only two pitches although Mr Horton's connections have ensured some high-class performers have graced this ground. A mature tree has been left inside the playing area at around mid-on or backward slip and there is a slight slope on the far side from the hall. It is lovely setting with the important church of St Matthew in the background. The first game was played here in 1999.

MORTON

Back Lane

Here we have a former pit ground with a grassed spoil heap forming a backdrop opposite the pavilion. A curious metal-framed fence with a curtain of industrial flooring painted white marks the boundary of this small, undulating ground. The pavilion is of recent vintage with a pitched roof and a scorebox attached on one end. There are houses all along this boundary. Beyond the grass car park to the right of the pavilion, is a handily placed public house (the Sitwell Arms). This is a ground that has increased in size over the years. The cricket club was formed in 1865 on a small parcel of land given to them by the Sitwell family, owners of the Brampton brewery. The brewery allowed them to increase the size of the ground in 1881 with a one hundred year lease at a peppercorn rent for the surrounding land not within the roped playing area. This lease was extended in 1981, at an increased stipend, by John Smith of Tadcaster who now own the pub and brewery.

NETHERSEAL

The Hawthorns, P.D.Richardson Memorial Field

The Netherseal St Peters club re-formed after the war and opened a new ground called the Hawthorns in the middle of a field to the East of Main Street. It was a square ground with a wooden fence around the whole boundary and was level and well kept. The small pavilion in the North East corner of the ground was, looking back with the benefit of hindsight, a considerable health hazard being constructed from asbestos. The village cricket and football clubs built a large, and still successful, clubhouse with a bar, function room and changing rooms for footballers, on the West side of Main Street in 1962. New housing planned to block off the access to the cricket ground and the cricket club agreed to move off in 1996. The fencing around the old ground has gone and it is an undistinguishable part of a large field. A new ground was constructed alongside Main Street on the opposite side of the road to the clubhouse called the Philip D Richardson Memorial Field (opened by Mr Richardson's widow in 1997). Unfortunately, the cricket club was dwindling in numbers and they hardly played on the new ground. It was used by Lullington Park's 3rd and 4th XI's in 2000-01 but the pleasant wooden pavilion has subsequently been burnt down by arsonists. The Richardson field is now used for football and the square has disappeared.

NEW MILLS
Church Road

New Mills cricket ground is accessed down a short, tight, lane off Church Road. There is an imposing gateway with metal gates inscribed with the name of the club that is different to the notice board next to the gates (the gates say New Mills and Newtown Cricket and Athletic Club and the board says New Mills Bowls, Cricket and Tennis Club). No matter, for this level, flat and almost square ground is an ideal small town sports facility. The cricket pitch is bounded by a path that leads to a pavilion in the far right hand corner (the floodlit bowling green is behind the pavilion with a disused rink close by). On the right hand boundary is a whitewashed brick wall with the Church and cemetery behind. An old wooden pavilion is now used as a tea room. The scorebox is directly opposite the pavilion. The ground was officially opened in May 1901 after the development of the Midland Railway had necessitated a move from an old ground next to the river behind Albion Road.

NEWTON SOLNEY
Behind Recreation Hall

Newton Solney cricket ground was acquired by a developer in the 1960's after the death of the local landowner Percy Ratcliff, who left the ground to the village, and it is now housing (one of the streets is called Cricket Close). As part of the deal, a new sports field was built by the developer further along Trent Lane. This is still a well-maintained recreation ground used by the children of the village but the cricket club, dating back to the dawn of the twentieth century, did not survive the hiatus between the demise of the old ground and the construction of the new ground. We understand that an annual match takes place between the two village pubs (The Brickmakers and The Unicorn) but no serious cricket was ever played on this ground. The old ground was used for grazing by cattle between games with the manicured square guarded by metal posts and a chain fence. There was a sloping bank for spectators at the Village Hall end of the ground and two small wooden pavilions (one for the home team and one for the away team) were located in front of the hawthorn hedge on the far side of the ground. The square was kept in immaculate condition but the outfield was rough and unkempt.

NORBURY

Mill Lane

A large field on Mill Lane with a tiny wooden pavilion once played host to both cricketers and footballers but, excepting the rather distressed pavilion, the only evidence of sporting endeavour is the single, rickety set of goalposts at one end of the field. The playing area would have been extremely uneven. Apart from the attractive hawthorn hedge that runs along the entire road boundary, the field is so large it is impossible to guess the size of the playing area.

NORTH WINGFIELD

King George V Ground

The King George V Ground at North Wingfield was once used for cricket by Ankerbold C.C. and Saltergate C.C. but both these clubs eventually departed to better grounds devoted exclusively to cricket and the game has not been played here since 1996. There are now two football pitches but the turf that formed the square is noticeably firmer underfoot than the rest of the ground. The pavilion is an ugly council building and there are houses all along one boundary. The park gates below the cricket field are quite nice with a unicorn on one pillar and a lion on the other.

OCKBROOK

Victoria Avenue

Ockbrook & Borrowash C.C. is the most successful club in Derbyshire over the past few years. They now have two pitches divided by trees and a ditch. The ground is located along Victoria Avenue, the main road that links Ockbrook with neighbouring Borrowash. The old pitch is leased from the brewery that also owns the public house next to the ground but the new pitch is wholly owned by the club, who developed it from agricultural land. The old pitch is rectangular and slopes downwards from the ditch to the main road. The worst of the once severe undulations have been flattened. There are practice nets and car parking in the spare land at the pub end of the ground. On the opposite boundary is a raised wooden scorebox that once had lethal steep steps at the back. Happily, the new steps have a nice gentle ascent. Curiously the new pitch next door slopes from top to bottom across the slope of the old pitch. Whereas the square on the old pitch is at right angles to Victoria Avenue, the square on the new pitch runs parallel to it. The square boundaries are much shorter on this pitch but conversely the straight boundaries are lengthy. However, it retains the rectangular shape of its elder brother next door. There are hedges on all the boundaries excepting the dividing ditch. The new pitch was dedicated to the memory of Richard Davison, a long-serving player killed in a car crash. The current pavilion, a bland wooden structure, is in the corner of the old pitch opposite the pub and extensions have been added to serve the new ground.

OSMASTON

Polo Ground

Osmaston Polo Ground, situated close to the church, village green and duck pond, is a venue with endless possibilities but it is likely to remain a 3rd XI ground for the foreseeable future. The ground was established around 1930 by the Walker family who had made their fortune in the brewing industry. The cricket ground is almost a perfect oval of fair size yet only fills around a third of the total playing area. The wonderful wooden pavilion painted burgundy and white stands back towards the centre of the ground so is somewhat askew from the cricket ground. It has a large portico with wooden bench seats running along the front and the interior has wooden paneling and a fireplace. There is a small scorebox dedicated to W.L.Foster who was a member of Osmaston C.C. from 1912 to 1969. The club folded in 1980 but a handful of friendly games have been played by a village team in recent years.

OVERSEAL

Recreation Ground

Cricket has not been played at Overseal Recreation Ground since 1990 when Overseal Phoenix C.C. left for Church Gresley. The main part of the cricket ground is now a football pitch. The square is still obvious because the middle section of the pitch is in immaculate condition. Either side of this area is rather boggy presumably as a consequence of lack of drainage past the hard compacted soil underneath the old square. The old wooden pavilion has been demolished and replaced with basic changing rooms for the footballers on the opposite side of the car park to the village hall and bowling green.

PALTERTON

Welfare Ground

The Palterton Welfare ground is still used for football but the cricket section was disbanded in the early 1960's. The ground is sandwiched between roads and housing but it is relatively spacious and level.

PARWICH

Royal British Legion

The Parwich Royal British Legion Ground situated off Creamery Lane is named Parson's Croft. The club disbanded in the 1960's but was reformed in 1985. A local farmer sold the original cricket field to the Parish Council and the game was happily revived in this idyllic part of the dales. The ground is shaped like the head of a mushroom with a small chunk missing in one corner where the end of a row of terraced houses projects into the playing area. The sycamore in this corner is a massive specimen festooned with ivy. A slab path leads from the car park to the Thornton Pavilion, a characterful building constructed of timber. Next to the pavilion is an artificial practice net (rubber) and the square has an artificial strip. A tennis court and bowling green next to the ground are almost totally obscured by a high hedge.

PEAK DALE

Recreation Ground

Peak Dale Recreation ground is still used for football. There is a short private road leading onto the ground. A large brick pavilion that was not designed to enhance the beauty of the Peakland views from the ground is pitched between a small car park and some kind of electrical installation. The dry stone wall on the western and northern boundaries is partially derelict and a wire fence has been erected to take its place as a boundary marker.

Cricket was played on this ground before the First World War and the team continued after the Second World War almost until the 1960's. A poignant sign in front of the field reads - "By order of Wormhill Parish Council No cricket, No cycling, No cars on the pitch & No dogs"

PEAK FOREST

Recreation Ground

Peak Forest Recreation Ground was a tiny ground and it has been further reduced by house building, tree planting and the construction of a playground on the far side from Hernstone Lane since cricket was last played here in the 1940's.

PILSLEY

Welfare Sports Ground, Back Lane

Pilsley Welfare Sports Ground was established around the last decade of the nineteenth century on the site of a long since demolished windmill. There is a cricket pitch, a full-sized football pitch, a football pitch for children and a bowling green. The welfare building, car park and bowling green run alongside Rupert Street and the pavilion is between the bowling green and the cricket pitch. The pavilion was erected during the inter-war period. Regrettably, the small, stand-alone scorebox was burnt and vandalized and the scorers now sit in the main pavilion. The ground slopes across and down from the road end but is quite substantial in size. There is a concrete strip next to the pavilion showing little evidence of use for practice purposes. The views from this plateau ground are far-reaching but the open aspect makes this a cold place to be in adverse weather conditions. This former colliery ground is now owned by the parish council and maintained by the district council.

There was a ground off Back Lane in the middle to late 1950's used by Ankerbold C.C. This land was part of the colliery but has now been converted to farmland. The sloping field that was used for cricket now has a large farmhouse in one corner and a bungalow in another corner. The old stone building used as the changing rooms still stands next to the bungalow but is in a state of disrepair. We are indebted to Mr George Astell, who owns the farm, for describing the layout. His father allowed Ankerbold to use the land and it is still known as the 'cricket field' to the members of his family.

PINXTON
Miners Welfare

The narrow but well-kept cricket ground of Pinxton Miners Welfare has now been commandeered for football. The pitch, which is dead level despite being situated up quite a steep incline, is fenced on all sides with banking on the path side. The steps and wall are all that remains of the old pavilion (the footballers change in the Welfare building below). There are contrasting views from this ground. Looking back toward the Welfare, the M1 motorway can be glimpsed but just above the ground, at the top of the hill, is a church and graveyard. The ground dates from the inter-war years and was funded by the Miners Welfare.

PYE BRIDGE
Riddings Ironworks

The cricket ground of Riddings Ironworks, last used in 1971, was alongside Main Road at Pye Bridge. The land was extensively opencasted but was subsequently reinstated in 1995 as the ground of Amber Valley Rugby Club. The old cricket pavilion was on top of the high bank opposite the current rugby clubhouse and the old steps are still visible. The oval cricket pitch was beneath the bank and is now split into rough grassland and the second rugby pitch.

QUARNDON
The Common

Quarndon is a charming village ground but hardly worthy of the tremendous standard of cricket maintained by the 1st XI of the club. Although the turf is in excellent condition there are some grotesque humps and hollows particularly below the square on the southern boundary. In fact, this ground slopes in all directions to varying, sometimes stomach-turning, degrees. The pavilion and scorebox is a long whitewashed building but the square is placed off-centre in the only piece of flat ground. A weather vane on the roof commemorates the victory in the 1983

National Village Championship. There is an old net opposite the pavilion but an impressive new facility is being constructed in wasteland at the bottom of the ground. There are numerous mature trees around the boundary and all the views, including that of the City of Derby stretched out in the distance, are pleasant.

REPTON

Repton School, The Moor

Repton cricket is generally associated with the famous public school and their excellent ground. The ground has changed in size and shape since it was originally constructed in 1845 or 1846 (the two main sources of information, Alfred Cochrane and F.R.Monro, disagree). It was a rough, sloping meadow and was leveled at a cost of £90. The whole extent was little more than two acres. The field was doubled in size in 1859 when a fence was removed from the northern edge but the outer edges were left rough until 1874 when the whole area was levelled. The field was increased again in the 1890's when a rough meadow to the North called Doctor's Paddock was incorporated. Final improvements took place in 1912 when another twenty yards were added to the field and the original pavilion of 1860 (described as 'unsightly' by Monro) was replaced by the current attractive building. The whole ground now constitutes approximately seven acres with two squares. The main pavilion is in the South West corner of the ground. It is placed on a bank with concrete steps onto the field. The roof is thatched with a clock tower in the middle. The second square to the North is served by a modest wooden pavilion. The buildings are separated, almost the whole length of the field apart, by a double grass bank with steps leading down from the school buildings. Opposite the main pavilion is a timber scorebox painted black. The ground is bordered by a wire fence on the northern boundary and a stone wall along the East and South boundaries as far as the main pavilion. There are six practice nets in the North West corner. The sightscreens at the pavilion end move along a fixed rail on the wall but the other end is served by orthodox sightscreens. The turf is in perfect order and the whole ground has charming views with open countryside to the North

and the school and town to the South. Apart from the school eleven, the ground has been used by Derbyshire 2nd XI and by the old boys' team, Repton Pilgrims.
The town team played on the playing fields down Broomhills Lane off Main Street. This lowly venue, particularly compared with the school, was known as The Moor or The Pastures. A small square is evident between two football pitches but the ground has only been used in recent years by 3rd and 4th XI's from out of town. The Repton club folded in 1967 and a team from nearby Milton played here until 1991. The changing rooms are modern but featureless.

RIDDINGS

The Park, Unwin's Field

The Park is off West Street and is a pretty ground. The sports field (football to the left and cricket to the right) is fenced off from the large car park. The straight boundaries are much longer than the relatively short square boundaries. On either side of the rather inelegant pavilion are mature oak trees (one inside the boundary and one outside the boundary). Opposite the pavilion, midway between the square and the boundary, is another mature tree, this time a formidable beech. Opened in 1847, this is one of the oldest continuously used grounds in the county.
Granwood C.C. played on a field at the rear of the Red Lion Inn. The team was active in the 1950's but the land, known as Unwin's Field, was used for new housing in the 1960's and no trace remains of this unremarkable ground.

RIDGEWAY

Sports and Social Club

The square on the Ridgeway sports ground is wedged between a full-size football pitch on the far side and junior football pitch at the bottom end. Lest anyone misunderstand the sporting priorities in this town, there is an artificial five-a-side football pitch next to the bottom football pitch. In addition to the poor outfield engendered by the winter game, the ground suffers from a severe slope up from the pavilion at the bottom. The changing rooms are housed within a modern redbrick community centre well below the level of the bottom football pitch. Some new trees have been planted on one square boundary but the other has an unbroken line of modern housing behind the hedging. The ground was bequeathed to the people of Ridgeway by the Hutton family at the end of the nineteenth century and it is run by trustees who rent it out to local sports clubs.

RIPLEY

Butterley Works, Butterley Hall, Mill Hill School

The Butterley Brick Company once funded a superb local cricket team and their ground is on Nottingham Road, Ripley. It was once prestigious enough to play host to Derbyshire 2nd XI but is now a bleak and bland public park. The team that plays here is still called Butterley (actually Butterley United) but the council now owns the ground. The old brick pavilion that sat atop a bank on the opposite side of the ground to the main road was demolished many years ago and the council has built windowless red brick changing rooms (two hexagons connected by a small corridor). The site of the old pavilion is now a skateboarding rink. The ground was smaller in its heyday but the old brook was removed and a field next to the ground has become a junior football pitch. This may be a good thing for local children but the cricket ground is now an uncongenial open space and the cricket pitch is uncomfortably sandwiched between football pitches. The fortunes of the team have waned over the years and the turnstiles that clicked over to welcome the paying spectator have been removed. The ground only has a low wooden fence to ward away the endless drone of traffic on the main road.

Butterley Hall was owned by both the Outram and Wright families, who were instrumental in the founding and running of the Butterley Brick company. The house was purchased by the police authority in 1969 and transformed into the headquarters of Derbyshire Constabulary. The extensive police sports grounds were opened in 1978. The cricket pitch shared an outfield with the rugby and football pitches. The grass square is gone and a rather threadbare artificial pitch is all that remains.

A typical, yawningly open, state school playing field at Mill Hill School was used by Ripley Amateurs in the 1960's and, more recently, by the indefatigably nomadic NEMCO XI between 1989-91. There are no permanent structures on the ground, not even a scorebox, and the changing rooms are part of the main school building.

RISLEY

Treetops Hospice, Approved School

Risley Cricket Club should be congratulated. They have converted a field into a good cricket ground within a decade. The ground is situated behind the Treetops Hospice off Derby Road. The field belongs to the hospice and the cricket club mows an adjacent field in return for the use of the ground. The small wooden pavilion has just been superseded by a larger structure obtained from Rolls Royce through the auspices of Birch Homes. Practice nets (one artificial and one turf) have been established and new trees planted on the only open boundary opposite the pavilion. The ground is quite small and the unseen noise of the A52, hidden behind the boundary opposite the entrance is the only jarring note to the rural atmosphere.

Until they moved onto their current ground, apart from a brief interlude on the Sandiacre Friesland School playing fields, Risley C.C. had played on the cricket ground belonging to the Approved School at Risley Hall, purchased and opened by Nottinghamshire County Council in the 1940's. The cricket pitch was part of eighteen acres of playing fields and was close to Risley's old ground behind the Blue Ball public house where they had played before the war. The school was closed and sold in the early 1990's and is now a luxury hotel and restaurant.

ROSLISTON

Strawberry Lane

Rosliston cricket ground is approached down Strawberry Lane. This is a ground that shares with football but both sports have their own facilities. The playing area is small with a tiny square. The old wooden pavilion has been replaced with a white Portakabin-type building. Rosliston Cricket Club only play Sunday friendlies and their close proximity to the splendour of Lullington Park will always militate against local players choosing to play at this rather prosaic ground.

ROWSLEY

Recreation Ground

Rowsley Recreation Ground on Peaktor Lane was opened in 1890. Unfortunately, this large and mostly flat ground is now only used for football. The 'Cuth Harrison Pavillion' (sic) has a double pitched roof with a verandah in front and there is some old cricket gear stuffed into the roof beams of the changing rooms. The football pitch is on the far side of the ground from the pavilion and the location of the cricket square is now impossible to determine.

SANDIACRE

Longmoor Lane, Crossley Premier, Sandiacre Friesland School

There is documentary evidence of a team representing Sandiacre as far back as 1814, possibly playing near the Plough Inn during the early years. The existing Sandiacre club definitely established their current home no later than the turn of the twentieth century. They adopted the name Sandiacre Town after the First World War to avoid confusion with Sandiacre Premier, the Crossley Premier works team formed in 1904. The ground on Longmoor Lane has been considerably upgraded in recent years. They have a new brick pavilion perched in splendour at the crest of the ground on the opposite side to the main road, three excellent practice nets with artificial turf and the undulating outfield has been levelled. The ground still has a steep slope but it is now almost perfectly even. The new pavilion, opened by Ian Botham in 2002, is all that a modern ambitious club could need but it is not as pretty as the old wooden building and the roof has some alarming kinks on the left side that ruin the symmetry of the façade. The former pavilion was constructed in 1902 and its simple predecessor was converted into the groundsman's hut. The playing area is much longer across than it is from top to bottom and is surrounded by housing on all four sides. This is mollified by high hedges on two sides and a row of trees along the bottom boundary that shields the main road and the houses behind on the bottom boundary. There is a drive from the small car park near the gate to the pavilion at the top.

The aforementioned Sandiacre Premier club were one of the leading teams in Derbyshire but their ground was over the

Erewash in Nottinghamshire, as was the adjacent ground of the Lace Web Company. However, to the South of these grounds wedged between the Erewash Canal and the River Erewash, is the former home of a later incarnation of the Crossley Premier works team (a separate entity to Sandiacre Premier C.C.). The ground, used around the 1960's, is long and thin with a railway carriage pavilion and a rusting roller remaining to remind people walking along the canal footpath that this was once a cricket ground.

Friesland School has an ample, banked, sports field behind the unprepossessing school buildings. The cricket square is turfed with one artificial strip. Naturally, in a modern school, the outfield is shared with football on both sides but there is a small scorebox on the far side of the ground from the school. This boundary is tree-lined and there are quite pleasing views of the countryside. The ground is used by Sandiacre Town 3rd XI.

A team of young men played together as Clouds Methodists in a rough, sloping field off Stanton Road. There were no permanent structures of any description and the pitch was a strip in the middle that had been given a good mow. This basic ground, and the club that played upon it, ceased to exist in the early 1960's when the M1 motorway was driven through the field.

SAWMILLS

Riverside Ground

This was the ground of the Stevenson's company (later to become Amber Dye Works) until 1976. It is located on Ripley Road and is now a football field with a playground near the gate. There are lots of dips all over the outfield and the turf is mole infested. This was a small ground when used for cricket and the playground has now reduced the playing surface so that cricket would be impracticable. There are rather nice views looking across and beyond the ground from the main road.

SCARCLIFFE

Rotherham Road

In recent years, Scarcliffe C.C. have played in Stanfree and Clowne but in the dim and distant past (actually the early 1950's) they had a ground of their own in the village. This was little more than a field on Rotherham Road diagonally opposite the Horse & Groom public house. No buildings were ever erected for either changing rooms or ground equipment and it is now an unremarkable field.

SHARDLOW

Dog & Duck

Shardlow Cricket Club, unlike many small village clubs, survived the Second World War and played until around 1951. Their ground was set back from London Road almost opposite the Dog & Duck public house. Nowadays it is part of Field Farm and is used for agricultural purposes.

SHIPLEY

Shipley Hall, Colliery Ground, Shipley Boat Inn

The Shipley Hall ground was built to impress by A.M.Mundy, a powerful local landowner. He levelled his haystack yard by transporting soil from the top to the bottom and the ground was opened after three years work in 1899. To reach the ground on the edge of Shipley Country Park necessitates a drive along woodland paths before emerging onto a tree-lined ground. The woodland backdrop behind the pavilion must surely rate among the glories of Derbyshire cricket. The South and West boundaries have mostly recent plantings and are more open. Shipley Hill, the site of the mansion from which the club takes its name, is the prominent sight to the left of the pavilion. Behind the boundary to the right are tennis courts and extensive woodland (the former Coppice Inn may be glimpsed through the trees). The ground has a pronounced slope from the hall end down to the tennis courts and from the pavilion up to the top end. All the slopes are fairly even and there are good-sized boundaries all around. The brick extensions to the original wooden pavilion ought to be more tasteful and noise from the American Adventure theme park (about half a mile away) can be intrusive. There is an artificial strip at the top end of the square and two new artificial practice nets at the top of the ground. Derbyshire 2nd XI played a number of games here between 1984 and 1990.
There was a cricket ground at the Shipley Boat Inn that predates the existing ground in the village. It was first used by Shipley

Amateurs C.C. in the 1870's but the last club to play there was Nutbrook in the 1960's. The Shipley Boat, located on the Nottinghamshire border near Eastwood, is now owned by a member of the 1970's pop group Showaddywaddy and has been transformed into a nightclub called MFN. The ground was partly swallowed up by an extension to the building and a new car park.
Also predating the existing ground was the old colliery ground situated near the entrance of the American Adventure. This was much reduced by a railway line in the 1890's but cricket was played here by Langley C.C. in the 1960's. The ground was further reduced when it was levelled and relaid in the 1970's and it is now a football ground with unsightly changing rooms raised above the pitch on a bank.

SHIREBROOK

Miners Welfare, Railwayman's Institute

It is reported that, after a brief hiatus, there has been a revival of cricket in Shirebrook on the Miners Welfare Ground off Recreation Drive. Despite the rather unpromising surroundings (spoil tips and old terraced housing), this is a good ground. The field is split into a cricket and football ground with a fence between the two. The wooden pavilion has terracing in front and a small separate scorebox alongside. The playing surface is level and in good condition. The ground was opened in 1899 but the Miners Welfare team were always seen as the 'poor relations' in the town to the Shirebrook Supporters Club.
The Supporters ground was next to the Railwayman's Institute on Langwith Road. Their nice wooden pavilion is still there but the football ground is now enclosed with a wall and this has cut into the outfield formerly used for cricket rendering the summer game virtually impossible. The bandstand that stood on the opposite side to the pavilion has been demolished although the octagonal foundations remain.

SHIRLEY

Park Lane

Shirley sports field is found along the narrow, hedge-lined Park Lane. There is a high hedge along the road boundary and the right-hand boundary but the other two sides are completely open next to agricultural land. The wooden changing rooms and tea room is virtually derelict and has been replaced by two portakabins in the left-hand corner of the ground. The cricket square has been obliterated among the mounds of thick grass that proliferate all over the field but summer league football is still played here. The ground was established in the 1930's on land owned by the Osmaston Estate but the cricket team did not survive the war. A village team was re-formed in 1960 but died through lack of numbers in the early 1970's. We understand that the ground will soon be revived by Brailsford C.C. for their 3rd XI.

SMALLEY

Stainsby Hall

Stainsby House in Smalley was demolished in 1972 and replaced with a Spanish-style ranch but the name of the building lives on through the cricket club, Stainsby Hall C.C. The club played in front of the house from 1863 by courtesy of the famous Sitwell family. The Sitwell's relocated the club to their current home in 1915. It is a compact, picturesque ground off Dobholes Lane divided from the car park by a bowling green and tennis courts (both recently revived after a few years of neglect). Looking out from the balcony of the pavilion in the far corner of the ground from the car park, to the right is a high hedge that protects the gardens of houses on Wilmot Drive. To the left is another hedge, lower than the opposite side with open fields behind. There is a public footpath between the boundary fence and the hedge on this side of the ground. The pavilion end boundary is lined with mature trees. The square has an artificial strip and the old practice net is now unused. The outfield is in excellent condition but contains a number of gentle undulations and slopes. The original pavilion was bought by Charles Stokes of Horsley Woodhouse for less than £2. The players had previously changed in the Sitwell Arms some distance away on Wood Lane. The Sitwell estate was dispersed after the death of Commander R.B.Wilmot-Sitwell in 1939. Appeals to buy the ground only raised an inadequate £10 but H.H.Dix, the headmaster of Smalley Boys School, bought it for £180 and leased it to the club for a peppercorn rent. Mr Dix's last act as Chairman in 1960 was to hand over the ground under a deed of trust and a new wooden pavilion was opened in the same year paid for by public subscription. This building has now been replaced by the splendid modern structure. The club has endured a traumatic period recently and, whilst members of the Premier League, they planned to rip out the hedges and enlarge the area of the ground to meet E.C.B regulations. Thankfully this plan has now been shelved and the ground retains a charming rural atmosphere, small yet prettily formed.

SMISBY

Park Place

Smisby cricket ground was a spacious field with a sharp slope up from Derby Road. Cricket was last played here by the village team in the 1970's. The field is now overgrown and the top half has been planted with Christmas Trees. The wooden pavilion, now demolished, was in the top right corner of the ground.

SOMERCOTES

Cotes Park, Viyella

The original Somercotes cricket ground was converted into a greyhound stadium and was abandoned by cricketers before the Second World War. The location of this ground is now occupied by part of the road into the industrial estate, a NHS Logistics Authority and the Royal Mail Alfreton Delivery Office. The council developed a new ground alongside the pit road off Nottingham Road. This was a level oval shaped arena with a wooden pavilion. Unfortunately, the council soon decided to sell the ground for industrial development and is now the site of the Pilkington Glass company.

A more enduring ground in Somercotes was that owned by the Viyella Company (formerly Aertex). The ground, now completely overgrown but essentially intact, is at the entrance to the factory off Hockley Way. There are steps up to the site of the substantial wooden pavilion near the gates. All that remains of this building is the concrete foundations. The ground had an odd shape in that three boundaries are straight but the other bulges out towards Hockley Way.

SOUTH NORMANTON

Jim Sims Memorial Ground, Frederyck Gent School

The Jim Sims Memorial Ground is a circular field at the end of Chestnut Drive. The ground was opened in 1991 and was constructed to provide recreational opportunities to the people living in the housing estate that surrounds it. There is a dreary looking brick pavilion next to the car park with concrete steps leading down to the ground. To the right of the pavilion is an overgrown concrete net and a playground set back in the bank above. On the far side of the ground there is a bank dropping down towards the houses. The square has an artificial strip and the playing surface is level and relatively flat.
Until they moved onto their bespoke ground, South Normanton C.C. used the playing fields of nearby Frederyck Gent School. These are the familiar, blustery, open spaces favoured by modern comprehensive schools with changing rooms located in the school buildings rather than a purpose built pavilion next to the pitches.

SOUTH WINGFIELD

Holme Lane

South Wingfield cricket ground is on Holme Lane. It was established around 1900. The club, founded in 1884, had previously played close to the ruins of Wingfield Manor. The pavilion, part of which dates from 1961, is at the top of the ground nearest the road. The wooden pavilion has an overhanging roof with a separate scorebox to the left. To the left of the scorebox is a patio area with benches and further along two impressive artificial nets. The square also has an artificial strip. The ground has an even slope apart from some undulations at the bottom end and is in good condition. The playing area is quite small with completely straight side boundaries and curved ends. The ground is enclosed by a moulded concrete fence. A raised railway embankment runs alongside the left-hand boundary and there are two football pitches on the far side of the meadow.

SPINKHILL

Mount St Mary's College

Cricket has been played at Mount St Mary's College, a Roman Catholic public school, since 1842. The principal field has been used since 1890. A big ornate wooden pavilion, slightly distressed, crowns the bank overlooking the flat, even, well-maintained field. The front of the pavilion has a metal balustrade painted white with steps leading down onto the field. There are two more cricket squares between a bewildering array of rugby and football pitches further away from the school buildings. The ground was used for friendly cricket in the 1970's by a team of villagers based in the Angel public house.

STANFREE

Oxcroft Miners Welfare

The cricket ground in Stanfree is situated next to the Oxcroft Miners Welfare. The Welfare is a new building (the old one across the road was destroyed by fire) and they own the cricket ground and the nearby rugby ground and bowling green. Scarcliffe C.C. moved here when they were ejected from Villa Park in Clowne. This is a ground built on old pit land and is banked on two sides. The playing surface is modest in size and slopes in varying degrees all over. The changing rooms are built into the welfare building. Opposite the welfare are newly planted trees that conceal the workings of the former drift mine.

STANLEY

Dale Road

The sloping rural ground of Stanley St Andrews C.C., dating back to 1894, could be approached along Dale Road in Stanley or down Hagg Lane in Dale. In either direction, a rustic road worsens into a bridle path. The club disbanded in 1970 and the ground is now an agricultural field. Whilst attempting to discover the whereabouts of this ground, our car was stuck in mud and the local farming fraternity were understandably hostile. We suggest that any curious cricketers should view this ground on foot or horse confined to the public bridle path (it is the lowest field at the Stanley end of Lower Hagg Farm).

STANTON

White Horse Inn

Stanton is just inside the border with Staffordshire in the South West of the county. The White Horse Inn had a field behind the pub and it was used for friendly cricket by the Craven Tasker works team in the early 1980's. The ground, which had a gradual slope up from West to East, is now derelict and overgrown with piles of burnt rubbish. A solitary goalpost remains standing to remind visitors that this was indeed a sports ground.

STANTON BY DALE

Crompton Ground

Stanton by Dale is the epitome of English rural cricket grounds. It can be approached from two directions. The shorter walk by the village pond is problematic due to the lack of car parking but the other route, from the car park of the Chequers Inn (a hostelry that actively welcomes cricketers) is tortuous and stile ridden (a real handicap with modern cricket bags). The ground itself is small and pretty with far ranging views unfortunately including the puffing chimneys of Ratcliffe on Soar Power Station. It is surrounded on all four sides by fields (arable on two sides, horses and sheep on the other two sides) divided from the completely level playing surface by concrete posts and wire fencing. The pavilion is brick built and modern with a three-door garage next door. There is an artificial strip on the edge of the square.

STANTON IN PEAK

Pilhough Lane

Tiny, bumpy, wavy, unforgettable Stanton in Peak cricket ground is located off Pilhough Lane. It is owned by the Thornhill family of Stanton Hall who have been benevolent landlords to the cricket club since 1870 although the current ground dates from around the beginning of the twentieth century. Dry stone walls surround the ground on three sides with a wire fence on the other boundary. It is a diminutive ground with a prodigious slope from top to bottom and the small square is the only level piece of land in sight. The wooden changing rooms (built in 1911) and tea room (1956) are rustically pleasant and placed in the top right corner of the ground with stone sheds and toilets to the right. Beyond the wire fence at the bottom of the ground is agricultural land and some spectacular views of the peak district. There is an elegant engraved stone giving the name of the club at the top of the unmade drive that leads onto the ground presented by the manager of a quarry.

STAVELEY

Miners Welfare, Staveley Works

The Staveley Miners Welfare ground is situated near the fire station off Lowgates. The large building on the site is the sports clubhouse but is almost as big as the Welfare itself on the other side of town. This is a large ground, even with a large chunk taken out on the pavilion side for an excellent tarmac car park. The outfield is generally level with some slight undulations particularly on the car park side. Trees shield the ground from the traffic on the main road on the far side and there are trees all along the River Doe Lea on the East boundary. The imposing clubhouse is mainly given to catering for social functions (the bar and tea area is vast) and the standard of the changing rooms and scorebox on one end are rather disappointing for such a good facility. Behind the pavilion boundary, a residential caravan site overlooks the ground and the St Johns Ambulance brigade have a hut on the ground. The square has an artificial wicket.

Cricket has not been played on the Staveley Works ground at Barrow Hill since 1988. The company was taken over by British Steel and the ground was sold to a private buyer. It is currently a golf driving range but the outer ring of the ground has been besmirched with tipping. The opening match was played on this ground in September 1952. It was an admirable sports facility that catered for cricket, football, hockey, tennis, bowls and athletics. The long, oval shaped playing area was overlooked by a fine wooden pavilion (now demolished) and surrounded by a running track.

STERNDALE MOOR

Hindlow Works

We believe that the Hindlow Works ground, at around 380 metres above sea level, is the highest ground ever used for cricket in Derbyshire. It is still used for football by Buxton Junior F.C. and is big enough to accommodate two pitches. The quarry is partially hidden by trees, the quarry road boundary is fenced and the opposite side has a dry stone wall. The traditional wooden pavilion, worth preserving with a nice verandah, is set back from the ground with a car park in between. There is a motor shed in the North East corner.

STONEBROOM
Birkinstyle Lane

Stonebroom may have the nastiest looking pavilion in Derbyshire. It is constructed from concrete and breeze blocks, covered with graffiti and resembles an inner city public toilet. A rotting wooden tower protrudes from the roof presumably housing the water tank. It is unfortunate that this pleasant ground has been scarred with such a building. The ground is entered off Birkinstyle Lane leading into a car park bordered by basketball courts and a football pitch that forms half the outfield. The square, in superb condition, hugs the touchline. The boundary lengths are adequate but the ground does drop away to a brook on the far side opposite the pavilion.

STONEYFORD
Boat Lane

Stoneyford Cricket Ground was close to the entrance of Stoneyford Lodge on Boat Lane. Apart from the memories of old men, the only indication that the field was a cricket ground is the curved corners. The playing area was long and narrow bounded by countryside with pleasant views. The ground was certainly in existence before the First World War and was used by Stoneyford M.W.C.C. until 1960.

STRETTON
Derby Road

Stretton had a cricket ground behind the village hall. The hall was built in 1947 on land donated by the Walkers, a public-spirited farming family. The cricket ground was beyond the lawn and tennis court at the back of the hall and was also owned by the Walker family. It was abandoned in 1973 and has now reverted to farmland. Even the location of the tennis court is barely discernible.

SUDBURY

Sudbury Hall, Sudbury Prison

Perhaps only Chatsworth cricket ground has a grander neighbour than Sudbury Hall cricket ground. Sudbury Hall (owned by the National Trust) is a wonderful house dating back to the seventeenth century and the cricket ground is on the opposite side of the road to the main façade of the hall. The ground is pretty with a rustic wooden pavilion set back in the midst of mature trees. It has a large playing surface with an artificial net on the opposite side to the pavilion. The square is off-centre towards the main road in relation to the pavilion.

The other ground in Sudbury has a rather less exalted backdrop – it is within the open prison that was opened in 1948 on the site of a former American Army Hospital Camp. The cricket ground was established around the same time that the prison was built. It was one of the first grounds to use artificial turf wickets and grass wickets have not been used for many years. The ground has very short straight boundaries but the square boundaries are quite adequate. The playing area is level but rather rough. A brick pavilion stands in the open corner of the ground with a high wire fence on two boundaries and saplings along the remaining boundary. There are pleasing views of open countryside looking out of the pavilion away from the prison.

SUTTON ON THE HILL

Sutton Hall

The cricket ground is situated in a field behind Sutton Hall (formerly a vicarage built around 1820) and was built around the early part of the twentieth century. It is entirely enclosed by a wire fence and hedging by the pavilion. The pavilion, moved from the ground at Longford, is a wooden structure with an attractive white-posted verandah. The ground slopes upwards from the main road with undulating waves across the entire outfield (mercifully the square is level). The boundaries are short by most standards, particularly so straight. The club only plays friendlies knowing that most leagues would be unimpressed by the standard of the facilities and outfield. Equally, the picturesque views with the hall prominent in the background make for a pleasant afternoon's cricket on a warm summer day.

SWADLINCOTE

Eureka Park, Thomas Wragg

At first sight Eureka Park is promising. This is a public park built between the wars on top of a colliery spoil heap. Tree-lined paths lead down to the sports field from the main road. Unfortunately the old cricket pavilion is gone, replaced by a horrible Portakabin, and the bandstand next to the ground has been levelled and capped with concrete. Fir trees divide the cricket and football ground from a bowling green and tennis courts but the overall impression is of a once proud civic facility in decline.

The Thomas Wragg works ground, a large multi-sport facility off Midway Road, is now completely submerged beneath the Poets Corner housing estate where all the streets bear the names of famous poets (Wordsworth Avenue, Shelley Road etc).

SWANWICK

Swanwick Hall

The cricket ground is part of the extensive playing fields of Swanwick Hall School. It has been restored as a cricket facility by the local club who have been playing on the ground since 1973 apart from a brief interlude at Markeaton Park in the mid-1990's when the League took exception to the lack of facilities (these problems have been substantially rectified). The pavilion is perched on a bank above the cricket field that is surrounded by football pitches on both sides. It is constructed of wood with a brick front. To the left of the pavilion are two rubber matting practice nets. The very small square is forced to the left of the pavilion by the football pitches. The square boundaries are long but a high bank shortens one of the straight boundaries. The appearance of the ground is pleasant with plentiful trees and the school in the background but noise from Derby Road is very audible. Swanwick Hall was purchased in 1920 by the Chesterfield Education Committee and was converted into a

Grammar School. The playing fields probably date from around this period.

SWARKESTONE
Barrow Turn

In the 1930's some young men were playing on a rather unsatisfactory cricket ground at Ingleby Lane. They drank in the Crewe and Harpur Arms and they prevailed upon the landlord to allow them to play in a field close to the public house at Barrow Turn just before crossing the historic bridge. The pub and ground was owned by the eccentric Harpur-Crewe family of Calke Abbey. The pavilion is charming but dilapidated with a ramshackle roof and a breezeblock WC alongside. There are two artificial nets and the playing surface is oval and flat.

TADDINGTON
Horse Mill Lane

Taddington Cricket Ground was a primitive venue away from the village located in a field off Horse Mill Lane quite close to the modern A6 road. The cricket club only just survived the war and organised sport was last played in this field in 1946. Despite the passage of the years, it is still possible to discern the location of the small square.

TIBSHELF
Newton Road

The sports field on Newton Road owned by Tibshelf Parish Council is capacious but the cricket pitch is rather cramped and impeded by a severe bank on the boundary next to the road. The square is placed between two football pitches and the outfield suffers accordingly. The pavilion, built in 1993, is a modern council facility and, as is usual with these buildings, is practical but unattractive. It does have a pitched roof and sits on a raised bank above the cricket pitch with a wooden scorebox alongside. Although the ground is next to the road and has housing on two sides, it is quite peaceful with mature trees dotted around all four boundaries.

TICKNALL

The Grange

Ticknall has much to recommend it. The ground, known as The Grange, is off Repton Road just outside the village with a superb modern pavilion on a bank above the playing surface. St George's Church is next to the ground on the opposite side to the pavilion providing a lovely vista for visitors. The ground has two artificial practice nets and an artificial strip on the square. Unfortunately the straight boundaries are extremely short for top-class cricket and the outfield on the church side of the ground is roughed up by the village football club who use the ground in winter. The ground is sloping but not undulating.

TIDESWELL

Recreation Ground

Tideswell recreation ground has some of the best facilities in Derbyshire. The Eric Simpson pavilion is an enormous stone building. A floodlit football pitch is behind the pavilion and there are some excellent tennis courts. There is another football pitch forming the lower part of the cricket outfield. Unfortunately the cricket area is mostly inadequate for top-class cricket. There is a heavy slope from the pavilion down to the square and then another big slope onto the football pitch behind the square. The main gates to the ground force a severe kink in the already narrow square boundary. High netting is forced to run along the Recreation Road boundary to protect the houses on the other side of the road. There is an artificial net in the top right-hand corner of the ground. All the weaknesses of this ground are topographical and the facilities and condition of the turf are first-rate.

TINTWISTLE

Speedwell

Tintwistle C.C. plays on the most Northerly ground in Derbyshire. It is located in the middle of a housing estate off a road called Speedwell. The ground would be square but for one corner sliced off nearest the road. The playing area is surrounded by a white wooden fence at the bottom and a whitewashed brick wall at the top end. The well-appointed pavilion is located in the top left-hand corner of the ground. This is a wooden building flanked by a scorebox and a tree. A garage and converted van body, undisguised to the left of the path from the car park to the pavilion certainly mar the appearance of the ground. The club claim a formation date of 1835 on their pavilion.

TISSINGTON

Recreation Ground

The cricket ground at Tissington that barely survived into the 1950's was tucked away from the 'picture postcard' village green on Chapel Lane. This was a long rectangular ground with an undulating outfield surrounded by dry stone walls and hedges. The plain chapel building is on the North western border of the ground. The wooden pavilion was dismantled and the only evidence of cricket today is a stone roller near what was the entrance to the ground on the southern boundary. The bowling green that was adjacent to the cricket ground has also disappeared without trace.

TUPTON

Queen Victoria Road

Ankerbold C.C. played at Tupton from 1963 until the 1990's. Found off Nethermoor Road, this was a large circular ground with a high bank curling around the southern end. The pavilion, a substantial social club building, looked over the ground close to concrete steps leading down onto the pitch. The building has been demolished and the ground is overgrown.

TURNDITCH

Windley Lane

Turnditch Cricket Ground was situated between the old Duffield-Wirksworth railway line and the River Ecclesbourne. This is now one large field with three trees in the middle looking up to the Old Bishops House on the hill. Walking across the area today, the first half is clearly of an agricultural ridge and furrow type field whilst beyond the trees, the cricket side is flat and still relatively even. The cricket field was generously proportioned with good views all around.

WALTON ON TRENT

Station Lane

The circular ground of Walton is almost 'in' the Trent as the river runs along the western boundary and as a consequence Staffordshire is only a big hit away. The pavilion is an impressive brick-built timber-faced building with a balcony. The boundary is encircled with a fence constructed with wooden posts and mesh. A willow tree stands within the fence in the North West corner of the ground. This is an attractive place to play cricket but the views are slightly marred by the close proximity of electric pylons with wires that snake across the open countryside towards Drakelow Power Station in the distance.

WESSINGTON

Road Nook Farm

The farming communities of Brackenfield and Wessington have played casual games of cricket on a number of fields in both villages. When they had a club registered with the Derby & District Cricket Association in the late 1960's, they played at the historic site of Road Nook Farm - it has a smithy dating from 1673 and a tithe barn of 1683. The rudimentary cricket ground is now a very coarse field populated by cattle.

WEST HALLAM

Beech Lane, St Wilfrid's Road, EMEB Sports

West Hallam White Rose C.C. have been playing cricket on Beech Lane since the 1880's. Unfortunately this is a ground that time has beaten. The short straight boundaries run into the road at one end and a housing estate at the other causing obvious problems. The shabby wooden pavilion is perched on a rise and looks out across the cricket field to a defunct football pitch (with a horrible pavilion) and the metal fencing of the Scargill School. The motor shed next to the cricket pavilion is extremely ugly. To their credit, the cricket club have recognised the irresolvable problems connected to their venerable old ground and are in the process of constructing a new one at Cock Orchard. Once this ground is ready, Beech Lane may continue as a third team ground for the club, for which purpose it will be entirely adequate.

The club were temporarily exiled from their long-standing home just after the Second World War when the prodigious slopes then prevalent on Beech Lane were levelled (soil was transported from the road end of the cricket ground to the football ground end). For two years the club played in a field off St. Wilfrid's Road kindly provided by the Southern family. The players changed in a huge marquee that was also supplied by the same farming family.

The E.M.E.B Sports Ground off High Lane East is a large flat ground in good condition. Nutbrook C.C., who purchased the ground from the Electricity Board, is a well-run club and they have constructed, with the help of lottery money, a spacious but unadorned pavilion. A rough road leads from the large car park to the pavilion, passing the dingy E.M.E.B social club building and some grubby chalets. This boundary is marked by a pleasant white picket fence. The ground is big enough to provide a substantial cricket arena and a football pitch on the far side to the pavilion (rented out to Mapperley F.C.) and the large area to the right of the pavilion is about to become another cricket ground for 3rd and 4th XI cricket.

WESTON UNDERWOOD

Park Farm

The home of Mugginton C.C. at Park Farm in Mugginton Lane End, Weston Underwood, is as bucolic as it sounds. It is on a plateau with splendid views of the countryside and is fairly open apart from a few trees and a hedge. The ground is shared with football but the long wooden pavilion, that replaced the old railway carriage changing room, is in front of the cricket pitch. The square is pitched at an unusual angle to the pavilion and there are some slight slopes and undulations, particularly on the cricket side of the field.

WHALEY BRIDGE

Horwich Park

Whalcy Bridge cricket ground, at Horwich Park, is reached by a tortuous route through narrow, steeply uphill, unmade roads that lead to a field occupied by cattle (the route begins as New Horwich Road in the town). It was first played upon in August

1883. A wire fence encircles the ground and the turf is in excellent condition. It is on a hillside so the only level piece of ground is the square. The slope is reasonably even with only slight undulations. The raised pavilion, constructed of metal sheeting in 1977, is in the top right hand corner of the ground and the pitched roof scorebox (dedicated to Jim Collier) is in the bottom right hand corner of the ground. There is a raised Portakabin to the left of the old pavilion that is used for changing rooms. Previous wooden pavilions had been built in 1905 and 1926. Whaley Bridge C.C. is moving to a more accessible ground in the near future. One can understand their reasons for abandoning this ground but it will be a shame to lose such an unusual and remote venue.

WHATSTANDWELL

Bent Hill Farm

Whatstandwell cricket ground was reached by a short walk off Carr Lane or a long walk down Bent Hill footpath from Crich. It was nearer the hamlet of Coddington than Whatstandwell. The ground was owned and maintained by a local farmer and the cricket ground was known as Bryan's Field. Mr Bryan, the farmer, killed himself in a fit of depression and his cricket field and wooden pavilion are no more. Even now, the turf is noticeably superior to that of the neighbouring fields and it is quite even. A dry stone wall runs around the field.

WHITWELL

Cricket Field Lane

Whitwell Colliery C.C. was formed in 1895. By 1904 they had built a new ground off Station Road on Butt Hill and became founder members of the Bassetlaw League. They are still members of the Bassetlaw League playing on the same ground. The changing rooms are good (a modern brick building with a scorebox in the roof), the outfield is even and manicured, the wickets are excellent and they have two artificial practice nets and an artificial strip on the edge of the square. Indeed, the only drawback to this tidy and well-maintained ground is the meagre size of the boundaries. There are walls and fences of varying types on all the boundaries.

WILLINGTON

Parish Playing Field, Power Station

There were two cricket grounds in Willington and both of them are now football fields. The town playing fields along Twyford Road is a large ground with trees along all the boundaries. The outfield is ridged apart from one area in the middle that we presume was the cricket square. The changing rooms are modern and ugly but this ground could still be restored to cricket. It was last used in 1980 by Willington Old Boys C.C.

An even larger ground, eastwards along Twyford Road, was once owned by the Power Station. This is now a privately owned by the Willington Sports and Social Club who have vague plans to develop a number of sporting activities currently limited to the omnipresent football (and snooker in the social club). This ground is on the opposite side of the road to the power station with the River Trent alongside the boundary. The profuse electric pylons are rather off-putting especially when they buzz in wet weather. Cricket was last played here in 1975.

WINGERWORTH

Deer Park

Deer Park School was built on top of the pre-war Wingerworth cricket ground but a new ground was opened in 1952. The new Deer Park has many things to recommend it; picturesque lakes on either side of the ground, excellent turf, tree-lined boundaries and a modern pavilion. Unfortunately there are an equivalent number of problems. The square is pushed up towards the school end to allow for a football pitch (no longer used) on the Longedge Lane side of the ground. The short boundary also has a severe drop towards the pond and a notable rise up towards the pavilion. The changing rooms are ludicrously cramped and the architect ought to have been quietly taken away and shot.

WIRKSWORTH

Recreation Ground, Anthony Gell School

Wirksworth men have played cricket since at least 1757 when the Derby Mercury recorded a game against an eleven from Sheffield. According to White's Directory of 1862 the present club was formed in 1849 and they still play on their original ground.

It was originally known as Broad Meadow and was owned by the Duchy of Lancaster. It was acquired by Alfred Arkwright in 1886 who purchased the ground in order to present it to the town as a cricket ground in perpetuity. Although Mr Arkwright died before this was accomplished, his daughter carried out his wishes and it was gifted to mark Queen Victoria's Diamond Jubilee in 1887. The Recreation Ground, as it is now known, is on Derby Road with a narrow drive past the football pitch that widens into a car park behind the cricket pitch. A concrete and metal rail fence separates the pitches. The ground slopes from the pavilion and car park down to the bottom but the turf is generally even and in good condition. The pavilion is stone faced with a verandah and an unusual reverse mansard roof. The timber part of the current pavilion was built in 1888, funded by public subscriptions and fund-raising events at a cost of £450. There are superb modern nets on the far side of the pavilion. On the other side of the pavilion are three benches set amidst six mature Scots pines. There is a bowling green hidden behind a hedge at the bottom end of the ground.

The playing fields of the Anthony Gell School were used by a team representing the County Office Staff. This team does not exist anymore and neither does the cricket ground. All that remains are three concrete strips, formerly used for cricket nets, next to the newly constructed Wirksworth Leisure Centre. The school is developing a new cricket ground that is expected to open in 2005.

WOODVILLE

Burton Road, John Knowles

The Woodville C.C. ground is located on Burton Road and is not likely to win many prizes for 'best in show'. It is flanked on three sides by a busy main road, an industrial estate and a modern housing estate. The pavilion is an uninspiring flat-roofed pre-fabricated type building. From the main road the ground has a severe but even slope to the flat square, but then slopes down to the bottom with hollows and bumps. It must be difficult to mow and a nightmare to field upon.

Woodville's other cricket ground was on the opposite side of town and was formed, owned and used by John Knowles Ltd whose factory was on the opposite side of the road. The ground is only just inside the Derbyshire border on Occupation Lane and is now used exclusively by Ashby Wells Football Club although the shape of the ground betrays its former usage.

YOULGREAVE

Alport Lane

Youlgreave sports ground is on Alport Lane. A car park runs parallel to the main road and is divided from the football pitch by a low stone wall. A high stone wall runs behind one end of the football pitch that doubles as the outfield of the cricket pitch on one side of the square. The pavilion is on the left of the ground level with the cricket square. This is a tripartite pavilion with the old central part opened by Ian Buxton, Captain of Derbyshire C.C.C., in 1971. The scorebox on the near side of the pavilion is dedicated to Peter Hill (a former player and treasurer of the cricket club) and was opened by Kim Barnett in 1993, as was the changing room extension on the other side of the old building. The ground has a severe slope after the square and the boundary is partly defined by three large trees. The ground continues behind the tree to a stone wall with a play ground to the left. A nice mature ash tree in a garden opposite the pavilion is rather overshadowed by a mass of leylandii in another garden.

APPENDIX A - BIBLIOGRAPHY

Where the title of the publication does not indicate how it has been useful for the purposes of this book, we have noted in italics the subject matter or geographical area. A number of websites have also proved invaluable, mainly, but not always, those of cricket clubs. Most of the books below were either missed by Padwick or published after the most recent edition of his monumental bibliography so listing them may be useful to future scholars of Derbyshire cricket. Does anyone fancy undertaking a definitive history of recreational cricket in the county?

BOOKS

The Buildings of England - Derbyshire: Nikolaus Pevsner, second edition revised by Elizabeth Williamson *(Churches and Houses)*

Derbyshire: Roy Christian *(General)*

The Derbyshire Country House (two volumes): Maxwell Craven & Michael Stanley *(Houses)*

A Long Time Gone: Chris Pitt *(Racecourses)*

The Trees of Britain and Northern Europe: Alan Mitchell

Hamlyn A-Z of British Football Records: Phil Soar

A History of Derbyshire County Cricket Club 1870-1970: John Shawcroft

Derbyshire County Cricket League 75th Anniversary: Mike Carey (Ed)

A History of the Bassetlaw & District Cricket League: G.R.Langdale

A History of Abbotsholme School 1889-1989: Derek Sederman

Around Alfreton: Alfreton & District Heritage Trust

Ambergate C.C. Centenary: L.Spendlove

History of Ashburne Grammar School: N.J.Frangopulo

The Spirit of Belper: Adrian Farmer

A History of Bolsover Colliery C.C: S.B.Fox

Walking Round Borrowash: Marion Johnson

Buxton College 1675-1970: R Bolton King

Calver A Booklet for the Millennium: Julia Beswick & Eric Wilkes

113 Not Out: D.W.Shimwell *(Charlesworth)*

Junior Cricket Reborn in the Seventies: C.R.W.Suttle *(Chesterfield)*
Queen's Park The First Sixty Years: Geoff Sadler
Clay Cross The Third Selection: Cliff Williams
The History of Clifton Cricket Club 1867-1967: George J Corbishley
The Story of Cutthorpe: S.Botham
Derby Congregational Cricket Club 125th Anniversary Supplement: Bernard Baines
Royal Institution for the Deaf & Dumb, Derby: Dr W.R.Roe
History of the Pastures Hospital: G.H.Gordon
Normanton Barracks Remembered: Normanton-by-Derby Local History Group
Where Heather Blooms on Ladylow: Jenny Nicholson *(Dove Holes)*
Doveridge Cricket Club Year Book 1957-58: J.H.Crosskey & J.Peacock
Haunting Visitations: Mick McDermott *(Dronfield)*
Three Ducks on the Trot: Don Woodhead *(Eckington)*
The Portrait of Edale: The Edale Society
Elvaston Cricket Club One Hundred and Fifty Not Out: Gordon Flint (Ed)
Tales of the Crimson Rambler: D.W.Shimwell *(Glossop)*
History of the Glossop Cricket Club: H.O.Hodgett
Old Glossop Cricket Club A Brief History: Derek Slack
Grassmoor C.C. 1884-1984: The Club
Hathersage Remembered: Bob Dawson and Ryland Clendon
Heage in Old Photographs: George Sparham and Walter Street
Holymoorside Past & Present: Ronald Entwistle
The Story of Ilkeston Rutland Cricket Club: Frank Blasdale
Langwith C.C. 1890-1990 A Centenary of Cricket: Robin A Brewster
The History of Cricket in Long Eaton, Sandiacre & Sawley: Keith Breakwell
Tuppence Up Penny Down: M.J.Arkle *(Matlock)*
Nottinghamshire Cricket Grounds: Peter Wynne-Thomas
Memories of Ockbrook & Borrowash: Marion Johnson
Repton Cricket 1865-1905: A.J.H.Cochrane
Repton Cricket 1901-1951: F.R.D.Monro

Rowsley 1849-1999: Ron Whitehead
The History of Shipley Hall Cricket Club: Simon Lacey
Around Shirebrook: Geoff Sadler
Smalley Remembered: Margaret Aitken
The Essential Works Order: F.B.Taylor *(Spondon)*
Stanley Parish and Area History: S.T.Lee
Echoes of Stanton Cricket: Harold Waller
Around the Wooden Box: D.M.White & J.W.Storer *(Swadlincote)*
The Whaley Bridge Cricket Club History: The Club
Wingerworth Landscape: D.G.Edwards
Wirksworth C.C. Centenary: Brian Hilditch

ANNUALS

Derby and District Cricket Association Handbooks (1947-1953)
Derbyshire County Cricket Yearbooks (1954 to present)
Derbyshire Cricket Association Directories (1980-1997)
Nottinghamshire and Derbyshire Border League Handbooks (1921-1980)
Derbyshire County Cricket League Handbooks (1981 to present)

NEWSPAPERS & MAGAZINES

Ashbourne Telegraph
Buxton Advertiser
Derby Evening Telegraph
Derby Mercury
Derbyshire Life and Countryside
Derbyshire Times
Heanor Observer
High Peak News
Ilkeston Advertiser
Ilkeston Pioneer
Ripley and Heanor News
Wisden Cricketer

WEBSITES

multimap.com
old-maps.co.uk
picturethepast.org.uk

APPENDIX B – STATISTICAL SURVEY

TYPE OF GROUND

1) Ground leased or owned by a private club
2) Grounds that are part of a public park or shared with other sports
3) Grounds established by collieries or miners welfares
4) Grounds established by companies
5) Grounds established by institutions
6) Grounds established by educational establishments
7) Grounds associated with a country house

STATUS

A) Used in 2003 or with a pitch still usable (e.g. visible square or artificial strip in reasonable condition)
B) Field with no use other than farming
C) Used for other sports
D) Partly or completely built over

	A)	B)	C)	D)	Totals
1)	58	42	5	15	120
2)	46	4	31	2	83
3)	13	2	10	4	29
4)	13	10	13	24	60
5)	8	4	3	6	21
6)	23	4	11	6	44
7)	11	3	1	0	15
Totals	172	69	74	57	372

APPENDIX C – GROUNDS USED BY DERBYSHIRE C.C.C.

GROUNDS IN DERBYSHIRE USED FOR FIRST CLASS CRICKET

Blackwell Miners Welfare
The Park at Buxton
Queens Park at Chesterfield
Saltergate at Chesterfield
County Ground at Derby
North Road Ground at Glossop
Town Ground at Heanor
Rutland Recreation Ground at Ilkeston
Recreation Ground at Long Eaton
Recreation Ground at Wirksworth

Grounds at Burton (three different venues) in Staffordshire and Dore in Yorkshire have been used for First Class cricket.

GROUNDS IN DERBYSHIRE USED FOR LIST A LIMITED OVERS CRICKET

The Park at Buxton
Queens Park at Chesterfield
Station Road South at Darley Dale
County Ground at Derby
Town Ground at Heanor
Rutland Recreation Ground at Ilkeston
Trent College at Long Eaton
School Ground at Repton

Grounds at Burton, Cheadle, Checkley, Knypersley and Leek (all in Staffordshire) have been used for List A Limited Overs cricket.

GROUNDS IN DERBYSHIRE USED FOR 2ND XI CRICKET

School Ground at Abbotsholme
Christchurch Meadows at Belper
Colliery Ground at Bolsover
G.I.C. Ground at Borrowash
The Park at Buxton

Queens Park at Chesterfield
Colliery Ground at Creswell
Station Road South at Darley Dale
Eyes Meadow at Duffield
North Road Ground at Glossop
Town Ground at Heanor
Rutland Recreation Ground at Ilkeston
Trent College at Long Eaton
Butterley Works at Ripley
The Field at Shipley

Grounds at Burton (two different venues), Cheadle, Dunstall and Knypersley in Staffordshire have been used for 2nd XI cricket. The Steetley Works Ground at Shireoaks in Nottinghamshire was used for a home fixture in 1978 but was later played on as an away fixture against Nottinghamshire.